GUNS N' ROSES AT 40

Guns N' Roses photo session at Roy Wilkins Auditorium, St. Paul, Minnesota, December 17, 1987. The classic lineup, left to right: Duff McKagan, Slash, Axl Rose, Steven Adler, and Izzy Stradlin.

GUNS N' ROSES AT 40

MARTIN POPOFF

CONTENTS

INTRODUCTION

Chaos has always reigned with Guns N' Roses, and the various forms of bad blood coursing through the guys' veins always seemed to spill over to the fan base, through rumors, through lurid headlines, through actual onstage rants and antics. It just feels like from day one it was always those guys against the world, the press, fans, potential fans, lapsed fans . . . we're a complaining bunch when it comes to Axl and Slash, that's for sure, or worse, Izzy and Steven.

But then something happened along the way. Throughout all the bickering and backstabbing, the guys, one by one, cleaned up and rehabilitated their images, to the point where there's really only one complaint left: the lack of enough new music. The funny thing is that gripe started about spring of 1989, in what seemed like a long and ragged ramp-up to the *Use Your Illusion* albums. It's comical now, how we were pulling our hair out, when you look back and realize that since 1991, there's only been *Chinese Democracy* with any meat on the bones, and even that's one of our industry's most amusing debacles.

Speaking of *Use Your Illusion*, that's the subject of a fond memory for me. I had only recently moved to Toronto and was this town ever epic when it came to the dispensation of physical product back when that was a thing. At Yonge and Dundas, basically Canada's main intersection, you had HMV and Sunrise Records, and probably still at that time an A&A—these were the big, flashy corporates. There was Vinyl Museum and a couple other grimy spots for used records, and I believe the Kelly's (where I bought the first two Budgie albums on a family van trip in 1977) was long gone by that point. Anyway, when the two *Use Your Illusion* albums came out, it was a case of drop everything and get downtown and scoop those up. Sunrise was offering a free T-shirt if you bought both, and HMV, right across the street, was going with buy one for $13.99, get the other one free. I opted for the HMV deal and then those two CDs became the talk of the industry and all my buddies for months, along, of course, with Nirvana's *Nevermind*, which was issued the following week.

Other fond memories are getting to meet the guys in the band and interview them over the years, usually Slash and Duff, never Axl. But let's go back

to *Appetite for Destruction* for a moment, shall we? I bought that at Track Records in Vancouver for $6.99 new when it came out. I had just got my first job fresh out of MBA school, working for Xerox in Vancouver (it still blows my mind that Duff went and got his MBA), and soon it would be all about grunge, kicked off for me personally when the *Screaming Life* EP showed up at Zulu Records a couple months later. At the time, I was into the Minneapolis scene, the new weird stuff from California, all things metal (every last goddamn album, actually), and yes, a constant supply of hair metal too.

Funny thing though; *Appetite for Destruction* was put in front of me and I remember it squarely as a hair metal album, albeit the best one. I mean, you flip the album over and see that picture of the guys, it's on Geffen, check out that band name, they are from Hollyrock, it sounds like dirty Aerosmith— why would you not think this is just another hair metal album? Digging deeper, I had every heavy punk album from the '70s, and any of this guff about the band's knowing punk or being into punk . . . I either never read about it, or if I did, I dismissed it. What I'm saying is I never made any sort of connection to punk with these guys, nor to any grand tradition like the Stones, although, sure, baby Aerosmith—absolutely.

In any event, that's my recollection. And then as grunge took over my consciousness, and hair metal got put in amber, *Appetite for Destruction* took its position in my head as the first of a short-lived "dirty hair metal" subgenre, sort of late-stage capitalism before the collapse. It was the first and the best example of a polluted bloodline that coursed through L.A. Guns, Faster Pussycat, Skid Row, Badlands, Seahags, Dangerous Toys, Cats in Boots, and Love/Hate, to name the most notables. Then Cinderella, Poison, and Mötley Crüe got in on it. Although the Crüe kind of set things up for Guns N' Roses in the first place: *Girls, Girls, Girls* beat *Appetite* to the draw by a few weeks, and the previous albums were in this wheelhouse too. The self-titled album from '94 marks a further evolution in dirty hair metal, but by then, everything had changed.

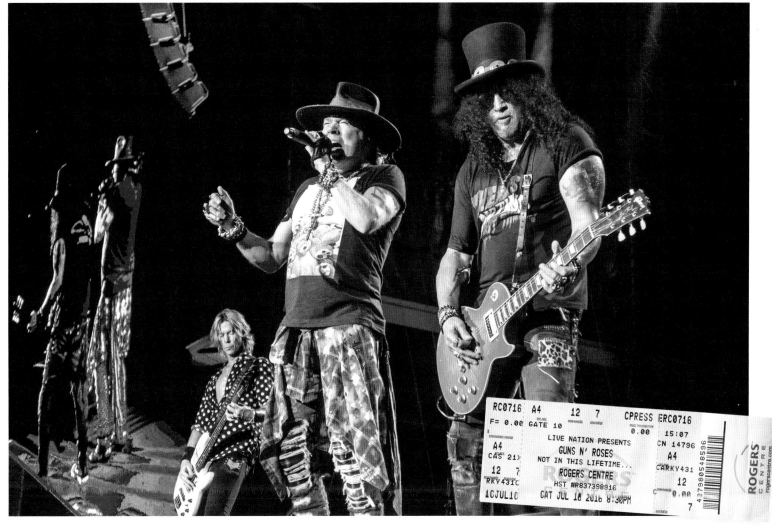

But the legend of *Appetite for Destruction* just grew and expanded and never stopped. I want to add that much credit for the phenomenon should go to the two *Use Your Illusion* albums, and the insane fame extension afforded. I always find myself defending the band against the grousers who say that GN'R are living off the glory of that one album. Because here's the thing: the two *Use Your Illusion* albums amount to essentially three albums worth of material. There's *GN'R Lies* and a covers album, and then dribs and drabs of new music here and there, plus the long, elaborate, ambitious *Chinese Democracy* album. And then it's true that Axl isn't exactly prolific, but Slash and Duff have made tons of new music when there wasn't a Guns. If you think about it, putting down Guns for not putting out is putting down the guys, and really, that's not fair. Even Izzy Stradlin, Gilby Clarke, and Matt Sorum are on a pile of albums.

So, the one complaint we're left with, after all the drug- and booze-fueled bad behavior, I don't think is valid either. We've got a ton of music from these guys, even if the name on the tin has been different. And if you learn anything from this book, it's that the battles always have been intense and visceral, that Guns N' Roses were the real deal, and that chaos indeed reigned, constantly threatening to destroy the empire. The fact that they ever got anything done is something of a miracle.

My satisfaction in doing this book then is that by the time we get to the end, I'm liking these guys as people way more than I did at the beginning, or I'm definitely less scared of them. And in tandem, in the same way *Appetite* took some time to catch on, I love that the Guns N' Roses catalog has lodged itself into my consciousness from such casual and not overly enthusiastic first baby steps. I've also enjoyed how the legend has grown to the point where, like AC/DC after *Back in Black*, they have become a band owned and embraced and beloved by the world, to the point where we can all enjoy them as one big happy dirty hair metal family, together, but at the same time, safely from a distance.

–Martin Popoff

The Not in This Lifetime tour hits BC Place, Vancouver, British Columbia, September 1, 2017.

SQUALOR ON THE SUNSET STRIP

1

01
NEW ROSE
Hollywood Rose forms

The end game is fame nearly beyond reason, but Guns N' Roses began modestly enough, the usual and haphazard way bands tend to happen, especially in a city with so many hungry singers and guitar slingers up and down the Sunset Strip.

The tale begins with Jeff "Izzy Stradlin" Isbell, moving to LA from Lafayette, Indiana, in 1980 and getting down to business with early bands like Naughty Women, the Atoms, and Shire. Flash-forward to 1983, where Izzy and local guitarist Tracii Guns find themselves commiserating over the business in the parking lot of the Rainbow Bar and Grill. Tracii introduces Izzy to his friend Chris, who is looking for new partners, given that Tracii at this point is concentrating on L.A. Guns. Chris and Izzy convene in Izzy's living room the very next day to jam some riffs. The two are soon joined by William "Bill Rose" Bailey, who, in December

Axl performs with L.A. Guns at the Troubadour in Los Angeles, October 5, 1984. Left to right: Tracii Guns, Axl, Rob Gardner, and Ole Beich.

of the previous year, had hitchhiked across the country to escape getting chucked in jail again and try his luck in Hollyrock.

Rose's first band when he got to Hollywood was an outfit with guitarist Kevin Lawrence called Rapidfire, with whom he had recorded a five-track demo just the previous month. In any event, the first meeting between Chris, Izzy, and Axl takes place in June 1983, on a black-tarred apartment building roof under a baking N' boiling California sun, and a new partnership is instantly forged, putting Rapidfire in the rearview mirror.

Fortunately, Weber's parents owned a house in Laurel Canyon that could become the new band's first headquarters, and within six months, January 1984, the guys found themselves at a now-gone sixteen-track facility recording a demo. Tracked were the songs "Killing Time," "Anything Goes," "Rocker," "Shadow of Your Love," and Reckless Life," with Izzy and Chris sharing the bass duties, supported at the rhythm end by a drummer named Johnny Kreis, hired through *The Recycler*.

Next came gigs, first under the name AXL. The band's lead singer, then going under the name Bill Rose, began adopting this band name into his own name and Axl Rose was born. AXL then became Rose and finally Hollywood Rose. Helping the guys quickly get a foothold was future (and short-lived) GN'R manager Vicky Hamilton, at this point working for a booking agency. Although the first date under the new partnership was at Madame Wong's supporting Candy, a more fateful booking would come later, when Hollywood Rose found themselves supporting Stryper at the Music Machine. Also on the bill were Black Sheep, with Vicky introducing Axl to that band's guitarist, Saul Hudson, aka Slash.

The first group photo of Road Crew, taken at the Fortress rehearsal studio, Los Angeles, 1983. Left to right: Slash, Ron Schneider, and Adam Greenberg.

Indeed, the tale becomes a game of musical chairs. Significantly, Slash already had been in a band called Road Crew—named after the Motörhead song "(We Are) The Road Crew"—with childhood friend Steven Adler and punk rock bassist Duff McKagan, recently arrived from Seattle. Soon Chris Weber would be off to New York City, with Road Crew's Steven and Duff winding up in Hollywood Rose. Meanwhile in Slash's world, there'd be his famed and failed audition for Poison. If that's not confusing enough, Hollywood Rose would break up and then reform for a New Year's 1984/'85 show, now with Axl, Izzy, Tracii, drummer Rob Gardner, and bassist Steve Darrow. Speaking of bassists, preceding Steve in this role, often for the briefest of tenures, were the likes of Rick Mars, Andre Troxx, Daniel "DJ" Nicolson, and finally someone called Snake.

Following this, there was a very short-lived first version of Guns N' Roses, consisting of Axl, Izzy, Tracii, Gardner, and Ole Beich. Beich's story is a tragic one. After being fired from the band

L.A. Guns, with Tracii Guns on guitar and Axl on vocals, at the Troubadour in Los Angeles, October 13, 1984.

Road Crew, featuring Slash, plays a party at Mars Studio in Los Angeles, December 1983.

after just two rehearsals, the Danish bassist was found drowned in a lake back in Copenhagen in 1991, with heroin and alcohol found in his system. His parents believed the cause of death to be suicide, due to his substance abuse problems and lingering depression over his ouster from Guns N' Roses. Both Beich and Rob Gardner also had been members of L.A. Guns, as had, in fact, Axl Rose, after the first disbanding of Hollywood Rose.

Speaking of L.A. Guns, the role of Tracii Guns in all this is equally confusing as the Hollywood Rose story. To be sure, Guns actually was part of Hollywood Rose for a brief time, and his introduction back in the Rainbow parking lot set the whole narrative aflame in the first place. Arguably his lasting legacy is not that for a brief spell he wound up in an official early version of Guns N' Roses, but more so that his last name would be imbedded as the first half of that illustrious brand for evermore. Satisfying to Tracii on some level should be the fact that L.A. Guns found a significant degree of success, achieving two gold records, and also that his band was responsible for more than a dozen albums across the years, culminating in 2023's *Black Diamonds*.

For audio evidence of the above convoluted tale, there have been a couple of questionable pieces of product put out, specifically a Rapidfire EP called *Ready to Rumble*, issued in 2014, and a Hollywood Rose CD from 2004 entitled *The Roots of Guns N' Roses*. Ancillary to the tale is the 1985 *Collector's Edition #1* EP from L.A. Guns, on which you can hear Guns, Gardner, Beich, and their singer at the time, Mike Jagosz.

Or you could go directly to official records from the heroes of our story, Guns N' Roses. "Reckless Life" and "Move to the City" are both on the band's original EP and the rerelease version of it as half of *GN'R Lies*. "Shadow of Your Love" was rerecorded for the 1988 Japan-only self-titled EP and has recently been in the band's live sets. And finally, there's "Anything Goes," which appears on the most sacred of GN'R texts, namely *Appetite for Destruction* itself.

TUCSON Garden NITE CLUB
3 15 88
L.A. GUNS
STAGE PASS

02

RIGHT NEXT DOOR TO HELL

Guns N' Roses plays their first show

Call it a merger to smooth things over, but Guns N' Roses is formed when, as Tracii Guns explains it, the manager of L.A. Guns fired freshly hired singer Axl Rose from the band, and instantly, Axl comes up with a side project of sorts so that he and Tracii can keep moving forward. It's also a merger of necessity, of sorts, because Tracii, Axl, and Izzy were all living together. Both had realized Izzy was a songwriting asset and about the coolest guy they knew. Rob Gardner is the band's drummer, and on bass at this point is Ole Beich, who, as previously alluded to, lasted a couple of rehearsals. Beich, comparatively, was viewed as quiet, even sullen, and lacking in enthusiasm for the project. Additionally, he was said to be too much of a dyed-in-the-wool metalhead.

Not the case with Duff McKagan, who lived across the street and had lots of punk rock in him, proof being his stage name Nico Teen when he was in his first punk band, the Vains, back in 1979 at the age of fifteen. Next came the Fastbacks, the Living, the Fartz, and Ten Minute Warning, with McKagan playing, variously, drums and guitar in these bands. In LA, having already played bass with Slash and Steven Adler in Road Crew, it was apparent to the guys both that Duff was an excellent musician and that he had the personality to match.

Here's how Duff once explained to the author the amount of punk background that he brought to the band: "I was a punker kid. The first gig I ever played was opening up for Black Flag in 1979. I saw the Clash in 1979, so I liked them, and Buzzcocks, XTC, the Avengers. D.O.A. were one of my favorites. They were like Kiss to me when I was a little kid, and they were from right up the street in Vancouver. I loved the Saints, and that's cool you know them. You know, we made this thing for producers, Guns did, this compilation of songs, to show what we kind of wanted to sound like. It was the best compilation. It had Motörhead, Nazareth, the Pistols, and it had the Saints. Because we had that song 'Move to the City,' with horns, so we must have picked up some influence from the Saints.

"But I grew up with that, and then hardcore started happening and then I was into Black Flag, Circle Jerks, Minor Threat. And I was in a hardcore band called the Fartz. So, for me, when I moved down the Hollywood, to see even long-haired guys like when I first met Slash and Steven, when I met them at this restaurant out of this music newspaper, and these guys had long hair, you know . . . [laughs]. And they listened to W.A.S.P. and I'd never heard W.A.S.P.! So, it was kind of a culture shock to me. I came walking in and I had blue hair and Slash's girlfriend thought I was gay, because I had blue hair and it was short. Hanoi Rocks was also something I came down from Seattle to Hollywood with. They were kind of the new thing, new for America anyway. And that was a natural progression, I think, from punk rock. If you were a rocker at all, you'd go there."

But Duff includes Izzy Stradlin in this meeting of the minds. "Yes, because Izzy had come to LA, and he was in this band called the Atoms and he was also in this other band called the Naughty Women, which was a punk rock band. The cool thing about Guns at the early stage is that nobody battled. We just brought what we had to the table, and it just meshed. Nobody was questioning anybody else. We all started listening to everything, all kinds of music, from R&B to metal to old Nazareth to GBH. So, it was a very well-rounded band as far as listening to music went."

Back to this idea of a merger at the band name level, it's almost as if the magic of seeing those two words together—"guns" and "roses"—had put a fresh coat of paint on what had been a moribund story for two bands experiencing fits and starts. That was Axl's idea, with a flyer quickly drawn up to make it real, and a new excitement was palpable as soon as Duff jammed with the guys (it's Beich, however, who is pictured in that first flyer). That initial summit resulted in recorded renditions of "Think About You" and "Anything Goes," both of which showed up on the band's landmark album, as well as "Don't Cry," which was central to the *Use Your Illusion* project. The guys were so impressed with the results that they played the tape when they got together for their very first radio interview, broadcast two days before their debut show.

A print announcement of the upcoming show amusingly explained that "L.A. Guns and Rose" had "smelted down" to form "Guns and Roses" (sic). There was also mention of the late-night KPFK radio appearance. Day of show, the marquee read "L.A. Guns," but much of the gathering audience were friends of the band and knew that this was a new thing. Having prepared beginning at three in the afternoon, then it was time to rock the Troubadour, on a Tuesday night, March 26, 1985. There was a surprisingly large crowd of about 150 that had now assembled to check out the merger. The band, sufficiently lubricated from hours of preshow socializing, blazed through a high-energy set that included originals "Shadow of Your Love," "Think About You," "Move to the City," and "Don't Cry," in other words songs from the Rose side of the ledger and not Tracii's. Also included were covers of "Jumping Jack Flash," "Heartbreak Hotel," and, more obscurely, Rose Tattoo's "Nice Boys," which Axl dedicated to rivals Poison.

On hand for the show was L.A. Guns/early Guns N' Roses manager Raz Cue, who recalls that the band sold a lot of booze that night, with management so impressed that the guys were paid $300 for the gig, compared to an earlier L.A. Guns show, which garnered only a $100 payday despite the same-sized crowd. Victory at hand, this particular assemblage was not to last. Soon both Tracii and Rob Gardner would be out of the band and the classic Guns N' Roses lineup was born.

Hollywood Rose, with Axl, Slash, Steven Adler on drums, and Steve Darrow on bass (far left), perform a pair of shows at Madame Wong's on June 16, 1984 (main) and June 28, 1984 (bottom left).

Another Slash-drawn gig flyer depicts the Hollywood Rose lineup.

03
NICE BOYS
Slash and Steven complete the classic lineup

The name is almost there, June 6, 1985.

A ROCK N ROLL BASH WHERE EVERYONES SMASHED

TWO FREE ADMISSIONS WITH THIS FLYER

9000 SUNSET BLVD, SUITE 405, LOS ANGELES, CALIF. 90069

FOR BAND INFO SEND S.A.S.E. / AXL ROSE

TROUB. JUNE 6 · 10 PM

GUNS AND ROSES

PHOTOS: ✓ Chris Amouroux

Despite the drunken success of their first show, it was a few weeks before Guns N' Roses gigged again. By this point, cracks were starting to show and Tracii signaled his dissatisfaction by skipping out on three band rehearsals. Drummer Rob Gardner then quit, expressing that he and Tracii were a team, and if Guns was gone, he was gone—they never worked together again. Conversely, as Tracii saw it, Rob left the band because Rob's girlfriend had given him the ol' "It's me or the band" ultimatum. Then there's Duff's reading of the situation. He says that he had announced that the band was going to do a West Coast tour and that both Tracii and Rob balked at the idea, with Rob gone queasy about what he figured would be a debacle.

In any event, on June 4, 1985, old Road Crew mates Slash and Steven Adler were hired on. Steven hadn't been doing much, but, as alluded to, Slash almost ended up in Poison. In fact, he'd aced the audition and was called back twice. But then C. C. Deville showed up in high heels and with mile-high hair. Deville had hardly learned the songs he was supposed to jam with the band, but when Bret turned to Slash and asked him what clothes he was planning to wear onstage, Slash said, "This is it." Despite DeVille's less than Slash-like chops, Poison had found their guy.

As for Steven, the band weren't completely solid about his hire, alternatively auditioning and considering Nicky Beat, previously with the Weirdos and later with L.A. Guns, for the gig. But as soon as Steven put his hand up and said he would do the West Coast campaign on short notice, the band liked his gumption and he was officially in.

On June 6, 1985, the classic Guns N' Roses lineup lit into their first show, back at the Troubadour, venue of the debut lineup's first gig two months earlier. It's also the first gig by the band where we have a verified setlist, consisting of "Reckless Life," "Shadow of Your Love," "Jumpin' Jack Flash," "Think About You," "Move to the City," "Don't Cry," "Nice Boys," "Back Off Bitch," "Anything Goes," and "Heartbreak Hotel."

Instantly remarkable is the voice of Axl, an inhuman howl, powerful, world-beating, wholly elevating the band's thumping version of "Jumpin' Jack Flash." As we progress through the set, the band is a freight train, heavy rock but both bluesy and intriguingly punky, low-slung and cool, and all attitude. Axl doesn't talk much, and the guys have no reservations about tuning up and otherwise idling between songs. Steven's drum kit was your basic John Bonham–type setup, dominated by a massive bass drum, and Slash was using his distinctive red B. C. Rich Warlock—this is also the guitar he took to his Poison audition and it would also be played on *Appetite for Destruction*. Halfway through the set, "Don't Cry" slows things down, but then it's back to more patently traditional heavy rock 'n' roll, ending off as traditional as possible, with Elvis Presley's "Heartbreak Hotel," albeit rocked-up like Status Quo.

Izzy Stradlin and Slash perform at what is considered the band's first official show at the Troubadour in Los Angeles, June 6, 1985.

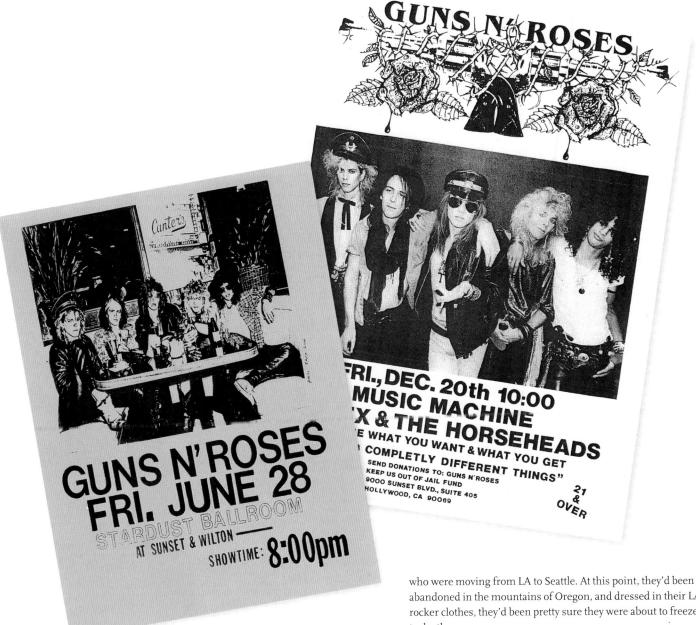

As for that West Coast swing Duff, what was later christened the "Hell Tour" indeed took place. Booked by the illustrious Duff, who had contacts up and down the coast and into Canada, the plan had been to play up to five shows in Seattle before working their way back down the coast and back to LA. The plan was to take two cars, but manager Raz Cue got sick and canceled out, staying home with his vehicle. One less body, the decision was made to hook a U-Haul to the big Oldsmobile owned by the mother of the band's roadie, Danny Birall. Seven people and the gear worked their way upstate until the transmission gave out near Bakersfield. The decision was then made to have the band hitchhike north with their guitars, and the gear to follow once the car got repaired. Izzy recalls that at that point they were next to a red onion field, and he started eating onions while going through heroin withdrawals. They soon caught a ride with a trucker high on speed who could take them only so far before he had to beg off and get some sleep. Next the guys were picked up by some girls

who were moving from LA to Seattle. At this point, they'd been abandoned in the mountains of Oregon, and dressed in their LA rocker clothes, they'd been pretty sure they were about to freeze to death.

Arriving at the venue, the guys found out that their equipment hadn't made it, so they had to use the gear of legendary punk band the Fastbacks, who were supporting. In front of an indifferent crowd estimated as low as ten and as high as thirty, the band played badly and was stiffed at the end of the night, denied their promised $250. As Duff recalls, after threating to burn the venue down, the band managed to get paid, with the manager calling the police and the band escaping quickly. Word then got around Seattle of the fracas—there was also an after-party where shots were fired—and the follow-up gigs in town were canceled, as were shows slated for Eugene and Portland in Oregon and San Francisco and Sacramento in California. They never did see their gear, and, as Izzy recalls, they had to steal a car to drive back to LA.

FRESH FROM DETOX

Photo: Jack Lue

GUNS "N" ROSES
'Rehab Show'   Sat. July 20
𝕿𝖗𝖔𝖚𝖇𝖆𝖉𝖔𝖚𝖗
8:30PM
$2.00 off with this ad

For Band Info:
SASE to 9000 Sunset Blvd. Ste.405 W. Hollywood, CA 90069

Another shot from the first official show finds Duff looking quite punk rock. Note, too, Steven's iconic drum kit and Axl's equally iconic kilt.

04
PRETTY TIED UP
GN'R signs with Geffen

The band played "My Michelle" for the first time at this Troubadour gig on January 4, 1986.

Having been convinced to go check the band out at the Troubadour, Geffen executive Tom Zutaut saw fit to offer Guns N' Roses their first record deal, officially acquiring the act on March 25, 1986. However, savvy as the guys were, there were games and demands, and playing off one suitor against another, with Chrysalis representing one of the more colorful stories.

"David Geffen didn't really participate in the scene that much," explains Vicky Hamilton, again, early-days manager of the band. "He trusted his three geniuses. That was Tom Zutaut, Gary Gersh, and John Kalodner. I mean, John Kalodner was pretty much the king of that stuff. He started out as a photographer, but then he was instrumental in the signing of AC/DC and Foreigner and some of the early bands on Atlantic, and worked with Led Zeppelin, as did Jerry Greenberg. But when they started Geffen Records, it was like John Kalodner was on Whitesnake and Aerosmith. And Aerosmith was Guns N' Roses' favorite band and instrumental in Geffen getting Guns N' Roses, because Tom Zutaut took them all over to his house and played Aerosmith records all night long, and the next day they announced to me that they wanted to sign with Geffen, even though we had a showcase coming up. I think it was four or five days later, and I had already confirmed twenty A&R people for the show [laughs]. And he offered me a scouting job at Geffen. I mean, Tom Zutaut was very good at getting what he wanted. And David pretty much trusted his A&R people—they were a very A&R-driven company. David Geffen was my biggest teacher, and I idolize him still to this day. I wish I had more of his business smarts, but no, he was brilliant. But I worked under Tom Zutaut, mostly."

Slash, Steven, and
Izzy backstage at the
Roxy Theatre in West
Hollywood, California,
prior to a sold-out gig,
January 18, 1986

"That's not exactly true," muses Zutaut, picking up the story when asked to verify Vicky's story around bonding with the guys over Aerosmith records. "We bonded over a lot of things, including punk bands like the UK Subs and the New York Dolls. They came over to my house, and we just spun a bunch of vinyl, all our favorite things, and it ran the gamut from Aerosmith to Thin Lizzy to Sex Pistols to UK Subs and all these more obscure British punk bands, all the way to Elton John. Axl was a big Elton John fan and Bowie fan. So, there was a bonding over music, but it wasn't necessarily just over Aerosmith. The Aerosmith story that probably got sort of distorted by the time, wherever you heard that from, was that they went over to Chrysalis Records, and the head guy at Chrysalis Records in A&R didn't know who Steven Tyler was. The band was kind of astounded by that, so they just kind of said to the girl working there in A&R and wanted to sign them, that they could never sign to a label where the head of A&R didn't know who Steven Tyler was unless she took her clothes off and walked naked down the street from her office to Tower Records on Sunset. Then they would sign with her because it would prove that she was a bold person."

In the meantime, Axl had asked Zutaut for a check for $75,000 by Friday, which was a ridiculous request. Still, Zutaut wanted the band, and he managed to come up with the goods, hoping that news wouldn't arrive that some gal from Chrysalis is walking down the street naked. In the end, the deal was for $250,000. But the agreement almost blew up a second time when Axl accused someone of stealing his contact lenses so he couldn't read the contract. His contacts were soon found, and Slash calmed him down and helped push the deal to fruition. Slash says in his autobiography that once he got his share of the advance portion, he quickly went and spent much of it on heroin.

As the saying goes, "You break it, you own it," so now it was up to Zutaut to herd these alley cats into the same place at one time, whether that was Rumbo Recorders, where they couldn't get it together, or the apartment he procured for them on Fountain Avenue, also where they couldn't get it together. More successful was the search for a new manager after Hamilton was unceremoniously cast aside, even if Tim Collins (Aerosmith), Arnold Stiefel (Rod Stewart), and Randy Phillips (now with AEG Live) all took one look at these guys and fled the scene. Left

A bird's-eye view of the January 4, 1986, Troubadour gig. Note that drummer Steven Adler is moving up in the world (literally), playing on a riser.

holding the bag was a buddy of Zutaut's, namely Alan Niven, who had already been through the wars with Mötley Crüe. But yes, now signed, Zutaut was the band's babysitter, so to speak, arranging all this stuff, managing them for a spell when there was no manager, trying to push the project forward after ill-advisedly having given them money.

"They were the authentic bad boys," confirms Zutaut, with a chuckle. "If we look at it in context, Guns N' Roses were like what the Rolling Stones were to the Beatles. Guns N' Roses were that to all the '80s metal bands. And they had way more punk. You know, they were basically like a dangerous bunch of drug addicts living a true, hedonistic, 'Fuck everybody and everything,' sex and drugs and rock 'n' roll lifestyle. And they were in it just to destroy the establishment in any way they could—physically, mentally, with their music, whatever it was. But they carried over a lot of punk ethic from the Pistols and other punk bands from the '70s. So it was that mix of metal, hard rock, and punk that made them

different. But then they were also the bad boys like the Rolling Stones were to the Beatles, and so that's why it was so infectious. The machinery was cranking out metal like Anheuser-Busch was cranking out Budweiser. It was just one unidentified metal band after another with one-hit wonders. And when Guns N' Roses came out, they were the dangerous bad boys, and people just flocked to it because it was so different, with all that punk in it."

Zutaut also liked the fact that they were songwriters, crafting their own songs. "To me, Aerosmith ceased to be a rock 'n' roll band when they started writing songs with Diane Warren. They turned into a pop band. You could still go to the shows and have a good time and stuff, but I think when these bands started using outside writers, they were turning into pop bands, and that was the end of that. None of my bands ever did that. If they couldn't write a great song, I didn't let them make a record. I just kept them out of the studio until they had ten good songs."

DIAMONDS IN THE ROUGH

GUNS "N" ROSES

Saturday · August 31st

THE ROXY THEATRE
w/ St. Valentine

For Band Info:
SASE to 9000 Sunset Blvd. Ste.405 W. Hollywood. CA 90069

Photo: Jack Lue

Left to right: Slash, Duff, Teresa Ensenat (Geffen Records, A&R), Tom Zutaut (Geffen Records, A&R), Axl (seated), Steven, and Izzy, backstage at the Santa Monica Civic Auditorium after opening for Ted Nugent on August 30, 1986

The most extensive demo sessions leading up to the recording proper of *Appetite for Destruction* took place under the guiding board-work of legendary Nazareth and guitarist and producer Manny Charlton, in early June 1986. Charlton is no longer with us, having passed away in 2022 at the age of eighty, but he left us with a pile of great music, most significantly seventeen albums with Nazareth from the beginning in 1971 through to 1989. As alluded to, Charlton did a fair amount of knob-twiddling for the band as well, most pertinently on the 1975 hit album *Hair of the Dog*, a record quite admired by the guys in Guns N' Roses, most notably Axl. What follows is the story of how Charlton was almost collared to produce what turned out to be one of the biggest-selling albums of all time, as told to the author back in 2007.

"What happened," begins Charlton, "was that Tom Zutaut, who was A&R for Geffen at the time, he called me up early in 1986 and said that he was signing a new band called Guns N' Roses, and I was under consideration for production, Axl being a big Nazareth fan; he's a big Dan McCafferty fan. So, one thing led to another, and I went over to LA to meet them. He had given me a bunch of cassettes, you know, straight board mixes, and to be honest, it sounded pretty useless. I mean, you've got to understand, they were nothing at this point. They were nobody. And also I was in the middle of recording an album with Nazareth. So anyway, I went over and met them and said, 'Listen, these cassettes, I can't get a handle on what you're doing, really. I can't hear the vocals properly. So why don't we just go into the studio, and you guys set up like it's a live gig and just record your set? And we'll do it straight to stereo. There'll be no multitracking, no overdubs, and we can do that in a couple of days. And then I'll be able to get a handle on your material.'"

particularly his first choice, or that he particularly thought I was a great guitar player or anything [*laughs*]. I don't think he was quite as big a fan as Axl was. But right from day one, I had the impression that Axl kind of ran the show."

This leads one to wonder if the big ol' N' in Guns N' Roses is a bit of a tribute to Nazareth, who similarly used the conceit in some of their album titles. "Maybe, maybe. We did that N in there all the time; we tried to get that in. I don't know; I don't think Guns N' Roses were thinking, 'Oh, let's do a Nazareth N' [*laughs*]."

The Demo Sessions

And at that meeting, was Slash perhaps wearing one of his top hats? "Yes. Yeah, very image-conscious. They all were."

And next came the music. "They played virtually everything that was on *Appetite*," explains Charlton. "They didn't have 'Sweet Child o' Mine' at that point. But they had several other songs, including 'Heartbreak Hotel,' which I don't think ever appeared on anything they did, but they did a great version of that. And 'Nice Boys'; they did a really great version of that. Two takes of that, actually. They also did a stunning version of 'November Rain,' with Axl playing piano and I think Izzy was doing some loose backing vocals. But that blew me away. When they did 'November Rain,' I said, 'That's a fantastic song, that's a great song, that should be on the album, that.' And Axl was going, 'No, no, no, that's for the next album.' I'm like, 'No, that's got to be on the first one! It's a hit! It's a fantastic song!' And of course they had 'Welcome to the Jungle,' which was stunning. I thought that was the best song they had at that point. But for 'November Rain,' Izzy was trying to do some loose backing vocals on it, but otherwise it was Axl and piano, and that's it. It blew me away. I

Nazareth guitarist and producer Manny Charlton, seen here in 1978, landed the gig producing the *Appetite* demo sessions.

had no idea he played piano so well. And the song was so well-constructed, great song. That and 'Welcome to the Jungle' were probably the two best Guns N' Roses songs ever.

"It went straight to stereo," continues Charlton. "There was no multitrack and there was no overdubs, so everybody just played. And Axl was between the two doors, in the studio. The two doors going into the studio acted as kind of the sound barrier, and he was in between the two doors, watching the guys through the glass and singing live at the same time. Those tapes are a very, very honest representation of what the band was doing at that time. There is no jiggery-pokery; there is no sampling or nothing like that. Just a straight band, and it was damn good. Loads of energy and lots of attitude.

"They did a couple of tries, but I don't think it was because of mistakes. I think it was because of tempo or something like that, that Axl felt it was too slow or too fast or something. And they did multiple takes of 'Nice Boys' and a couple of takes of 'Rocket Queen.' But most of the rest of it was pretty much straight through. I thought they were great. I just thought they were a band, with a capital 'B' at that point. They all seemed to be pulling their weight, and everybody seemed to be on the money and straight. They were good. It wasn't like I had to tell them what to play or how to play it. They just set up and played. Nobody was drunk. They were well together. Everybody was straight. Yeah, they were great at the time. Slash was outstanding, but Izzy was a solid player as well, and Steve and Duff were tight—they knew what they were doing. Super, super nice equipment too. All brand-new Mesa Boogie equipment and Gibson guitars; you know, I think there was money getting pumped into them. I think they were on some kind of development budget or something, although I'm not sure about that. At that point, I said to Tom Zutaut, 'They're great—really, really good.'"

For this legendary demo session, it was just Charlton and "the engineers in the studio, at Sound City. Tom [Zutaut] was in and out and in and out. He came in and had a look-see of what was going on and then he went away. And that was it. Basically, we did these tracks, the tape, and that's it. And I said, 'Look, I'm in the middle of an album with Nazareth, and if we could get our schedules to fit, put me up for the gig.' But they were trying different people at that point. They were talking to different producers. I think Gene Simmons was one of them. I think they were talking to him at one point [note: actually it was Paul Stanley that was considered]."

"Afterward, I went back to their flat with them and sat and chin-wagged for a while, had a chat. I didn't stay that long. They were there with their girlfriends and just sort of hanging out. So, I kind of felt odd man out. Just an apartment, you know. I think they all shared it. I think the five guys pretty much shared. It looked okay, looked comfortable, and clean. If they were into anything heavy, they kept it from me. They didn't let me see it. I found out they were pretty heavily into this and that, and when I asked them what they wanted to drink, when they came to my hotel and asked for a drink, Axl said, 'I'll have a Coke' and Slash said, 'I'll have a bottle of Jack Daniel's.' And I sort of raised my

eyebrow a little bit. But I thought they were just a bunch of guys. Maybe they had a joint or something like that, but that's about it, really, and beer. I don't think really at that point they could afford anything stronger [laughs]."

Looking Back

Underscoring his remarks about the band's preparedness, Charlton reflects that "Axl knew what he was doing. He seemed to have the master plan, you know? He seemed to know where they were going and what they wanted to do. But they wouldn't have done anything if it hadn't been for the record company. I think Tom Zutaut is more responsible for their success than just about anything else really. Because he really believed in them and nurtured them. I think he kept them alive at that point. Kept them alive with food and accommodation and stuff like that. It's not as if they were out making a lot of money at gigs.

"No, nothing. It was kind of like an audition," indicates Zutaut, asked if he was paid for his services. "Yeah, I think they thought that I was over there and I was going to stay there and do the job. But I made it clear to Tom [Zutaut] that I was in the middle of doing Nazareth, and we have to make our schedules fit—I was in the middle of doing *Cinema*, with Nazareth. We were recording part of it in the States, in Detroit, and part of it was done in Scotland, and it was mixed in England."

Asked if they at least flew him out for free, Charlton answers, "Oh yes. You want me to see a band, and I have to pay my own airfare?! I don't think so [laughs]. Accommodation, I paid for that myself. I was there for about three nights. It was pretty short and to the point. Like I said, I had to get back because Nazareth were in the middle of an album. But I went over there, I took a lot of time, I took some time out, and just basically I did a decent job. I got them set up and got them to play, and they were comfortable. And to me, that's what a good producer is. He's somebody who gets a performance. I didn't want to muck around with what they were doing—they knew what they were doing. I think they were pretty true all the way through. They had the songs pretty damn well arranged and played. Okay, the finished album sounded a little bit slicker and little bit more together, merely because they probably had more time to do it."

The extensive results of Charlton's work with the band can be heard on the massive Super Deluxe Edition box-set reissue of the band's sacred debut, issued in 2018, known as *Appetite for Destruction—Locked N' Loaded: The Ultimate F'n Box* (and to a lesser extent on the slighter version of *Locked N' Loaded* known as the Deluxe Edition). To be sure, these fascinating recordings suggest an interesting question—or game, or mental exercise—of "What could have been?" But really, in what world could the story of *Appetite for Destruction* have turned out any better?

05
PERFECT CRIME
GN'R issues *Live ?!*@ Like a Suicide*

Is faking an indie live EP the least punk rock thing a band could do, or is it in fact ridiculously punk rock? Ostensibly, *Live ?!*@ Like a Suicide* was the product of a band cranking out four songs in a rough 'n' ready live rock 'n' roll club situation and then putting it out on their own label, Uzi Suicide, a name that could have come only from a chaos magic ritual, or maybe a dungeon meeting of creepy gansta rappers. But the songs were done in a studio, Pasha Music House, in October 1986, and the record was pressed by Geffen. Indeed, the guys thought it was funny piping in massive crowd sounds from Texxas Jam, as if Guns N' Roses had ever played the Cotton Bowl, let alone ever been outdoors. But the chaos magic of the thing is miserably authentic, given the guys' dire drugging and drinking at the time, and it carried beyond the above factors onto the anarchic, nonsense titling, the cover shot featuring just two of the guys in the band, a logo designed by Slash along with haphazard text, and then the idea of picking two not particularly lovable cover songs to go with two not particularly lovable originals as old as Hollywood Rose.

Speaking to any sort of motivation that makes sense (beyond Duff playing four-dimensional chess with us), the idea was, in the main, cooked up by manager Alan Niven to fan the flames of a street-level buzz that was already sparked. Niven already had been there with an initial indie release of Mötley Crüe's *Too Fast for Love* debut, not to mention a preceding single. He'd also been there with Great White's first release, an indie EP with the same tracks on both sides. He'd also seen the power of distribution, being associated with Greenworld. He'd also been involved with Dokken, who had an indie EP and a weird release schedule of their *Breaking the Chains* debut. Furthermore, Ratt kicked things off with an EP back in '83, and that was legitimately indie.

Additionally, the idea here was to print up ten thousand cassette and 12-inch vinyl and copies of this thing, and all on black vinyl—the color counterfeits came later and likely from the Soviet Union. On the one hand, the plan was to send a bunch of promo copies of it to journalists in the UK, in advance of what turned out to be a three-day stand at the Marquee in London. On the other hand, Geffen could use the one-stop sale of the run—to Important Records distribution for $42,000—to finance this proposed promo campaign, creating a tidy closed circuit. Running parallel to this, the label brass at Geffen were starting to feel uneasy about the Gunners' collective appetite for destruction. *Live ?!*@ Like a Suicide* would be something Niven could place in their hands, a talisman representing progress. As for why it was concocted in the studio, Steven Adler remembers the label telling them it actually would cost too much to record the band live.

Booking agent John
Jackson and manager
Alan Niven photographed
backstage at the Monsters
of Rock, Castle Donington,
United Kingdom, August
20, 1988.

Axl gets down at the
January 4, 1986,
Roxy show.

In any event, the EP was issued on December 16, 1986, followed up with a release party at the Cathouse on December 23. Prying open the door and peering into the dankness and darkness, the first song we hear is "Reckless Life," co-written by founding member of Hollywood Rose, Chris Weber. Evoking the memory of *Kick Out the Jams*, Slash proclaims, "Hey fuckers! Suck on Guns N' fuckin' Roses!" and the band crash into an original that sounds like "Toys in the Attic" with less sophisticated chords. The guys steamroll through the song tight as a drum, and sure, let's say too tight to be doing this live, especially given their usual state of dishevelment. We hear Axl's voice for the first time and it's a fright. He tells us, pinched and frantic, that he's "reckless and feeling no pain." It's a punk rock lyric over a heavy metal backing track that nonetheless evokes the greatness of the Rolling Stones.

Next, when you've got an Axl Rose and a Duff Rose in a band called Guns N' Roses, you may as well cover Rose Tattoo, who are basically the Australian working-class version of AC/DC—across town, Great White went uptown, covering the Angels' "Face the Day." Amusingly, Steven plays the exact same thing on drums that we just heard nonstop for three minutes, while the rest of the guys launch into what is a fairly meat-and-potatoes pile of descending chords, augmented by some slide licks. Nothing flashy, the song elevates somewhat at the "Nice boys don't play rock 'n' roll" chorus refrain, to the point where the guys milk it with their fake Dallas, Texas, crowd.

The back half of the EP underscores the Aerosmith *Live! Bootleg* vibe of the opening track and sure, that of "Nice Boys" as well (by the way, Aerosmith headlined the first and most famous Texxas Jam). "Move to the City," a hard rock shuffle augmented with a distantly mixed horn arrangement, sounds like it could have been on Aerosmith's scrappy, scroungy debut from 1973. And "Mama Kin," covered here, actually was. But there's time for one last prank. The horn arrangement is an integral part to the original Aerosmith song, but Guns N' Roses say, No thanks, we kinda gave you that exact thing on the copy song we wrote ourselves.

Backstage at Fender's Ballroom, Long Beach, California, March 21, 1986, opening for Johnny Thunders. This was five days before the band secured their deal with Geffen.

06
GET IN THE RING
GN'R issues *Appetite for Destruction*

Geffen spent about $370,000 making *Appetite for Destruction*, a huge amount for a debut back in the day, but money that would be recouped several times over.

Izzy got thrown in jail for trying buy heroin, and Slash wasn't much better. Geffen president Ed Rosenblatt was about to drop the band. Hell, Tom Zutaut himself was going to do it. The guys had blown through their $75,000 advance long ago, along with an estimated additional $100,000, and this was after Zutaut already had learned his lesson not to give them money—just pay their rent and buy them food so they don't end up dead in the gutter.

Instead of firing the band, Geffen management decided to knuckle down and get the rest of the songs written that were needed for the album. These steps broke the cycle of inertia, got them to focus, and built some mystery. Axl says this almost killed the band, because it gave everybody more time to do heroin. Izzy affirms this, and adds that Axl's drug of choice was speed, which helped fuel the manic recording sessions that were about to take place.

One meeting with Paul Stanley, a potential producer of the record, went nowhere. As soon as he made some structural suggestions about "Welcome to the Jungle" and "Don't Cry," it was all over. The band, drunk on tequila they had just bought from over the border, got through the meeting but were put off. Even Steven, who was the biggest Kiss fan and bouncing off the walls about the summit, found cause to be offended. He was known for his minimal kit, with only a floor tom, a snare, and a prominent bass drum. Stanley suggested adding toms and even for Steven to think about going double bass. Steven had to admit Stanley was the wrong choice, but he still resented the band's disrespect toward his hero.

Bill Price, who had worked with the Sex Pistols, was considered, but there was no way Geffen was going to let the band go to London to record at Wessex. Jack Douglas was floated as a possibility, but Slash, a huge Aerosmith guy, was outvoted. Max Norman, a favorite of Zutaut, turned them down, considering the band not metal enough. Spencer Proffer also was considered, but his association with Quiet Riot was a bridge too far. Before Mike Clink was given the job, things only got serious with Manny Charlton (see sidebar on page 26). Clink hadn't done much producing, but he'd engineered with UFO, working with Michael Schenker, so he knew how to deal with guitars as well as difficult personalities.

Setting up shop at Rumbo Recorders for rhythm tracks and Take One for guitars and vocals, Clink and the band got the brunt of the work done over a couple months in early 1987, wrapping up, according to Axl, on March 27. But it was never easy. There were a lot of takes (though not excessive—Clink's particular skill is knowing when he had the right one), and the guys rarely worked together. When their presence wasn't required, they were off getting wasted, despite Clink strategically picking a place to

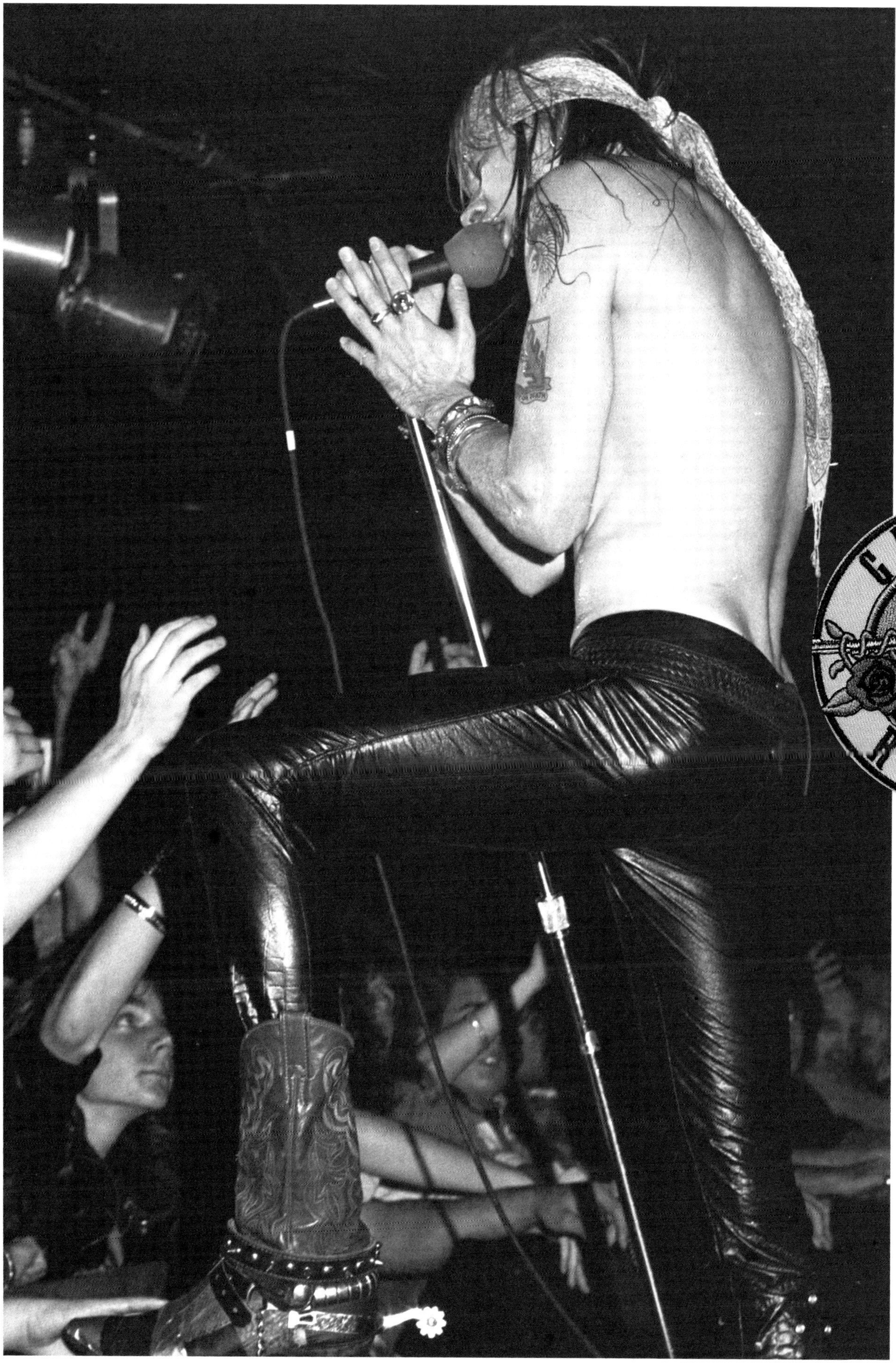

Axl at Bay Shore, New York, October 16, 1987

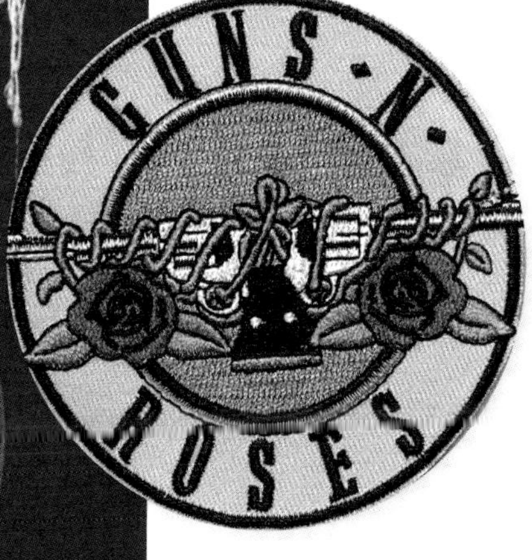

Slash at Bay Shore, New York, October 16, 1987. The band had just returned from a short string of dates in Europe.

work well away from Hollywood, where trouble was tenfold. Slash liked noon until eight (fueled on coffee and Jack Daniel's), and Axl would work from nine until three, keeping Clink and his engineer Micajah Ryan up at all hours, especially with Axl coming in increasingly late as the sessions wore on. Slash and Izzy had problems with heroin, with Slash having to cover for Izzy a fair bit on guitar and the guys resigned to using a lot of Izzy's scratch tracks. Steven wasn't partaking yet, so he and Duff were just drinking a lot. He also fondly remembers that his mom would bring the guys lunch and cigarettes and take their clothes away and bring them back clean.

For his part, Steven says he was done in six days, all the time fighting against the idea of playing to a click track and basically winning that battle. Axl, however, became obsessive about his vocals, to the point of recording a line or even a word at a time, and working alone in the middle of the night. The difference in temperament between all the guys and Axl was vast and resulted in an explosive chemistry once the record was done, with mixers Michael Barbiero and Steve Thompson also injecting their polar-opposite personalities into the final venom soup.

In the end, Geffen spent about $370,000 getting the record made, a preposterous amount for a baby band. It would of course be money well spent, or if not exactly "well spent," money that was recouped and more. Back on the battlefield, one might partly credit the magic of *Appetite for Destruction* to how much work Axl poured into the vocals, along with the obvious street credibility that bled into the songs, and then behind the scenes, the work of Zutaut, Clink, Ryan, Barbiero, and Thompson. Indeed, many elements push the record, either slightly or significantly, beyond other similarly configured records of the time. Some of these elements are quite abstract, like the quality and range of the vocals, the visceral sound of the guitars. Clink had a lot to do with establishing Slash's Les Paul and Marshall sound—the tightness of the bottom end, and the aggressive push and pull of Steven's combustible drum performance. Again, each member of the team worked differently, and much of it was a hot mess, but it all magically organized itself in the end.

"It's So Easy," backed with "Mr. Brownstone," was issued as an advance single on June 15, 1987, and *Appetite for Destruction* emerged on July 21, 1987, as just another major label hair metal album, albeit the first of a subgenre I'd come to call "dirty hair metal"—hell, in retrospect, not even the first, just the biggest and best. The point is, me an' my buds all thought there was something about the album that was "better than the rest," but that fuzzy opinion was elusive and fragile. As we'll see, the rest of the hard rock crowd was of roughly the same opinion: pleased but not doing cartwheels, given that *Appetite* proved to be the ultimate slow burner, entering a crowded field of good albums and taking months to really catch fire.

The band launched directly into controversy when they licensed the painting titled *Appetite for Destruction* by lowbrow outsider artist Robert Williams for the album's cover. After pressure from retailers, the label replaced the sleeve art with the now famous celtic cross and skulls.

"It's So Easy," backed with "Mr. Brownstone," was issued as an advance single. The 45-rpm 12-inch maxi-single seen here included live versions of "Shadow of Your Love" and "Move to the City."

ACT TWO
APPETITE FOR DOMINATION

07
ANYTHING GOES

GN'R's first North American tour

Celebrity Theatre,
Anaheim, California,
February 10, 1988

Yes, there was "Sweet Child o' Mine" and the Geffen machine, but much credit for the success of *Appetite for Destruction* goes to the blood, sweat, and tears that the band put into their sprawling and intense first tour. It was fourteen months of kills 'n' thrills, August 1987 to December 1988 with a light month here and there (March 1988 off), but otherwise appearing with hot hands like the Cult, Mötley Crüe, Alice Cooper, and most remembered, Aerosmith.

It all began on the down-low, as far away as possible, pretty much, in Halifax, Nova Scotia, a small city notorious for not getting shows. It was August 14, 1987, and the band was opening for the Cult, promoting their beloved third album, *Electric* (which, much like *Appetite for Destruction*, posed questions about what qualified as a Sunset Strip record). Axl might have picked up a few frontman pointers from Ian Astbury, but more materially, the Gunners would eventually abscond with the band's drummer, Matt Sorum. Guns N' Roses supported the Cult through to September 14, winding up in New Orleans.

Next came a short European leg with Faster Pussycat (a baby Guns N' Roses—there was a whole movement behind the Gunners building), followed by a return to America, where they played smaller shows on the East Coast, supported by Japanese Kiss pupils EZO (no opportunity to learn much there). October 23 found the band playing their first New York City date, at the Ritz.

November 3, 1987, marked the first of a notorious spate of dates with Mötley Crüe, at the peak of that band's druggy debauchery, six months after the release of their gormless and hapless hit album *Girls, Girls, Girls*. The pairing represented

GUNS N' ROSES
SUNDAY, SEPTEMBER 13, 1987
BRONCO BOWL AUDITORIUM
2600 FORT WORTH AVE.   DALLAS   8 P.M.
TICKETS ON SALE NOW ALL RAINBOW TICKETMASTER
LOCATIONS INCLUDING SEARS AND JOSKE'S.
CHARGE BY PHONE MASTERCARD/VISA METRO 787-1500

Duff, somewhere in the US in 1988. The whirlwind year also saw the band's first trips to Europe, Japan, and Australia.

a level of Dante's Hell beyond when the Crüe supported Ozzy Osbourne on *Bark at the Moon* in 1984. By the beginning of December, Guns N' Roses was supporting Alice Cooper and for the first time, the support act had a hotter album than the headliner, with *Appetite* climbing the charts and Alice promoting the garish *Raise Your Fist and Yell Record,* yet another album that asks who should be allowed to stalk the Strip (not Alice, or at least not yet). At the end of December at Perkins Palace in Pasadena, Fred Coury substituted for Steven Adler, who was out with a broken arm. On December 22, Slash was partying with the Crüe's Nikki Sixx when the bassist suffered his famous major overdose in which he died and was revived (Slash's girlfriend was with him as the paramedics arrived).

A series of smaller shows followed with the Gunners headlining, support coming from the likes of T.S.O.L., Zodiac Mindwarp & the Love Reaction, and U.D.O., further demonstrating the crossover taking place at GN'R shows. On New Year's, they shared the stage with Jane's Addiction.

With the band still gadding about town doing casual shows, Steven returned for a Cathouse gig in which the band was joined onstage by Vince Neil for their encore performance of AC/DC's "Whole Lotta Rosie." The band was good for a number of spontaneous covers over the tour, proving their worth as jammers. Regular parts of their sets included Dylan's "Knockin' on Heaven's Door," Aerosmith's "Mama Kin," and Rose Tattoo's "Nice Boys," but on occasion, the band would also play Alice Cooper's "Only Women Bleed," a second Rose Tattoo song, "Scarred for Life," and, best of the bunch, "Marseilles" by the Angels, along with

a big pile of tired old rock 'n' roll songs that don't warrant extra recognition—many were one-offs and sometimes played in part.

Now with a platinum-certified debut album, the Gunners were sent out supporting Iron Maiden, by then running on fumes with the recently issued *Seventh Son of a Seventh Son* album, a second dud after 1986's *Somewhere in Time.* It was the campaign supporting Aerosmith on that band's *Permanent Vacation* tour that entered rock 'n' roll lore. The tables had turned in several ways. First, Guns N' Roses were basically the new version of Aerosmith from exactly ten years ago, circa *Draw the Line,* always out of their heads, running on fame and fumes. Second was the huge irony that while Aerosmith were trying to stay clean, they were touring with a freight train of vice. Aerosmith manager Tim Collins remarked the Gunners were traveling like gypsies, with suitcases held together by string. The band was so out of it, he said, that the Aerosmith camp felt sorry for them.

The two sets of Toxic Twins would begin their partnership on July 17, 1988, playing together through September 15, where Axl and Slash joined Aerosmith onstage for the senior band's "Mama Kin." By this point, Guns N' Roses was generating more press and excitement than Aerosmith, although Aerosmith was about to go on a run arguably on par with what the Gunners would manage over the next five or six years.

Strength to strength, the circus continued, with a short trip to the UK, followed by the band's first tour of Japan, New Zealand, and Australia, in December 1988, where the band shared stages with the underappreciated Kings of the Sun as well as the Angels. When the Angels played the Whisky a Go Go the following year, Guns N' Roses joined the band for a rousing rendition of "Marseilles," with Axl shimmying, shaking, and clearly enjoying being shoulder to shoulder with the legendary and now sadly departed Doc Neeson.

08
PARADISE CITY
Appetite for Destruction hits #1 in the US

Released into the wild amidst worthy competition from bands both legacy and new, *Appetite for Destruction* didn't exactly languish, but nor did it take off like a rocket queen. Perhaps proving the unspoken premise that its ragged creators were from an older classic-rock tradition, it was taking it to the people that made it catch fire, along with lurid headlines and something else old-fashioned: hit singles.

The album only appeared on the charts a month after hitting the shops and a dozen shows into the band's first national tour, supporting the Cult, debuting at #182 on August 29, 1987. Across the next month, it had leapt to #142, then #100, and on September 26, reached #74. "Welcome to the Jungle" is issued as a single, but only in the UK, and the band continues to make waves live. Still, at one point, *Appetite for Destruction* actually slips in the charts, from #56 to #60 on Halloween of '87. Touring with Mötley Crüe commences, but the album languishes through this period, sitting at #56 as the guys switch over to shows with Alice Cooper and then closing the year out at #52.

By the end of February 1988, the album has executed a steady march to a #24 placement. After another month it hit #15, and then on April 19, *Appetite for Destruction* became certified platinum in the United States for sales of more than a million copies, getting there without crazy chart success or much of a push on the single end of things, given that all we've seen in the US is the advance issue of "It's So Easy," which didn't win hearts and minds. But a week before getting their plaques, the band filmed a video for their contentious ballad, "Sweet Child 'o Mine," and soon fuel would be added to the fire. If it can be said that an album can, again, "languish" in the top ten, *Appetite* indeed did that through dates with Iron Maiden, beginning the run at #9, rising to #7, and then slipping to #8. When "Sweet Child o' Mine" is issued as a single, on June 3, the album has slipped further, to #10.

At the legendary
Marquee Club in
London, June 28, 1987.

In a hot minute, Guns N' Roses will see the results of their up-tempo and sentimental southern rock song getting fed to the public, as the song begins its own ascent from a lowly #76 debut on June 25, 1988. Soon the band would tour with Geffen label mates Aerosmith and there'd be no looking back. By July 16, the album was at #5, the new single was at #50, and they'd just got word that the album had hit double platinum. The next day they opened their first show for the Boston bad boys, beginning a campaign that would put them on the cover of *Rolling Stone* magazine.

On August 6, 1988, *Appetite for Destruction* finally hits #1 on the Billboard Top 200, thirteen months after issue, with "Sweet Child o' Mine" serving as a microcosm of that journey, still fighting it out with pop posers at #18 two months after issue. A week later, the guys get word that the album has now gone triple platinum, and as the record slips a few spots on the Billboard grid, on September 10, "Sweet Child o' Mine" becomes the #1 song in America.

William Bruce Rose Jr. from Indiana basks in gold and platinum success.

09
DOWN ON THE FARM

GN'R performs at Monsters of Rock

Amidst Aerosmith dates and gathering Guns N' Roses mania, the guys were whisked across the pond on the Concorde to take part in 1988's Monsters of Rock festival, held at Castle Donington. Like Metallica experiencing their own Monsters of Rock tour as the future of rock on a bill with Scorpions, Dokken, Kingdom Come, and headliners Van Halen, the Gunners found themselves in similar mixed company stylistically, but comically down the bill with the hottest-selling album of the bunch.

Helloween, the faster, smarter, younger Iron Maiden from Germany, were to open the bill, beginning the long day at one o'clock in the afternoon. Guns N' Roses was next, followed by Megadeth, David Lee Roth, Kiss, and headliners Iron Maiden, who were the only band to play after dark. Despite the biggest crowd ever for a Monsters of Rock at 107,000, nobody on the bill was much of a commercial juggernaut on their own or at that point of their career. To be sure, this was Diamond Dave at his peak, but the peak was platinum. Megadeth could sell some records, but they were still four years away from their double platinum glory years. As for Kiss and Iron Maiden, well, both were living off past glories by 1988, although headline status is justly rewarded to those with long histories and attendant foundational credentials. Plus, Maiden were hosts, of sorts.

But to reiterate, Guns N' Roses had a triple platinum album under their belts, and it didn't look like the intense interest in the band was about to let up anytime soon. And they weren't some isolated US success case, which was the fate of many of the competing hair metal acts from LA at the time. The Gunners had played the UK very early, even before the first record, and they'd already made it a point to play UK on this tour. As well, "Welcome to the Jungle" had been a successful single there for many months, with "Sweet Child o' Mine" being issued in the UK to coincide with the Monsters of Rock appearance. The 1987 Kerrang! critics liked the band too, voting *Appetite for Destruction* the fourth best album of the year after records from Anthrax, Aerosmith, and Whitesnake, with the latter two acts being Geffen label mates of the Gunners.

Tragically, as the band hit the stage, the crowd rushed forward and in the mud that had formed from previous rainy weather, a "crowd collapse" of about fifty people took place. In an occulted evocation of Altamont (starring the Rolling Stones, spiritual heirs first to Aerosmith and then Guns N' Roses), Axl stopped the show as paramedics arrived to sort things out. Afterward, it was discovered that two concertgoers, Alan Dick, eighteen, and Landon Siggers, twenty, were killed in the crush, adding to the cursed legend of Guns N' Roses, although the band acted admirably at the time, pausing the show repeatedly, with Axl trying to exercise some crowd control.

There would be no Monsters of Rock in 1989, and afterward the crowd size would be limited to seventy-five thousand, along with some engineering to make sure that the area directly in front of the stage wouldn't be sloped, as it was on that fateful day back in the summer of 1988.

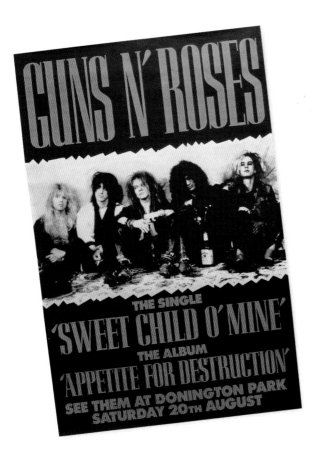

Slash and Axl hang with Lars Ulrich from Metallica and Dave Mustaine from Megadeth at Monsters of Rock, Castle Donington, United Kingdom, August 20, 1988. A few years after Lars tried on Slash's magic hat, Metallica would have a diamond-certified album—coincidence?

Appetite for Destruction

A DECONSTRUCTION

Given the record's enormous legend, it seems fitting to afford *Appetite for Destruction* outsize attention. Here's a little track-by-track breakdown of the album that put the first crack in hair metal, only for Nirvana to smash it to pieces four years later.

The record kicks off with what would be heralded as its masterpiece, an anthem for the ages called **"Welcome to the Jungle."** A vibe is instantly attained, a sort of hoodlum critical mass. There's cowbell, there's backing vocals, there's modulation and other sophisticated chord changes, but most of all, there's an immediate collective chemistry.

"We didn't know enough about studios to know to put a fuckin' vibe into a studio," laughs Duff, asked by the author whether they tarted up the room at all to help attain said vibe. "Really, our main concern was having some booze. You know, our main concern was getting songs down. We were really serious about our music. As long as we had a couple fifths of something, food wasn't really an issue. We really didn't care about what anything looked like. We didn't have naked girl pictures up or anything like that. I think we had a bunch of nasty magazines and stuff. This was a really nice studio. We didn't know you could put up anything of your own there. Had we known that, you know, we might have done something."

Swaggering like Aerosmith circa *Get Your Wings*, "Welcome to the Jungle" was fueled by guitars that cut through, instantly delivering that sound we now know as Slash's vital, urgent, timeless rock 'n' roll. Indeed, besides the almost novelty charm of Axl, enhanced by his deft and memorable use of stuttering, one is struck by the tone and attack out of the guitars. But Slash is not flash, his charm being this sense that he plays riffs N' runs very traditionally, but he plays them with his whole body.

"You're right, it's just his feel," muses Duff. "He wears his emotions on his sleeve when he plays guitar. You know, there's a guy like Zakk Wylde who will just rip your head off. And Zakk

is an amazing guitar player, no doubt about it. That goes without saying. Slash . . . like, my wife, on the way back from Vancouver one time, she's saying to me, 'What's the difference between a Slash solo and a Zakk solo?' And I said, 'Zakk will rip your head off and amaze you with technical ability.' There is perhaps nobody better at it. . . . Slash is more of a feel guy. Slash can make you cry with what he's playing. You know, ["Welcome to the Jungle"] was a song written about a time when Axl had hitchhiked, either in a part of Queens or Brooklyn or maybe even the Bronx, where these little kids were swinging sticks at him [*laughs*]. He found himself in this place where he just shouldn't have been. And then there were some old guys, you know, like, 'You're in the jungle, you're gonna die.' He's like, 'Fuck, let's get out of here.'"

For his part, Axl has related it's more about a trip to Seattle, with the sentiment being that you can get into trouble in LA, to be sure, but there's just as much vice to be found in a smaller place.

"Welcome to the Jungle" vaulted to #7 on *Billboard*, but only #67 in the UK, where it was nonetheless greatly spiced with a cover of AC/DC's "Whole Lotta Rosie" as its B-side. Its history as a single almost serves as a microcosm of the album's commercial arc, given that the UK release was in September 1987, but the US didn't see it as a single until October 1988. A collaborative effort by Slash, Duff, and Axl, its origins derived from an old Duff song called "The Fake," which he had put together as a member of the Vains back in 1978 (Duff has said it was the first song he ever wrote). The title, "Welcome to the Jungle," was lifted from a line in "Underwater World" on Hanoi Rocks' *Two Steps from the Move* album, that band's last record before their reunion (a major label release from 1984) and one of many influences on the Gunners.

"They were all old and washed up," says Duff, sensing the changing of the guard his band might signal. "I moved to LA in '84, and Hanoi Rocks . . . Razzle, their drummer, died in '85. I knew that punk rock was dead by '84. There was no scene. We were going to be the next. Us twenty-year-olds were going to be whatever was next, and it was very exciting. Punk rock was dead, metal was done . . . everybody was kind of a mash of all kinds of shit because of Hanoi Rocks and because of Mötley. I mean, Darby Crash from the Germs was dead. Black Flag got a chick in the band, okay? It's all done. It's over."

Next up is **"It's So Easy."** The song's dark, slashing chording, along with Axl's creepy, monotone vocal, just screams punk chaos, which, of course, suits Duff just fine. "With 'It's So Easy,' I had learned open E tuning from my next-door neighbor, West Arkeen," he explains. "So I wrote that song in open E and we recorded it on a little four-track."

Arkeen, a musician friend of the band, would die of a drug overdose in 1997. But before that, in the mid-'90s, Duff would record and play with him in side projects. Arkeen gets a co-write

SPEAKER CABLE
965

Of "Mr. Brownstone," Duff states, "Izzy came up with the main riff, and, yes, it's a song about heroin. And it was really prevalent within the collective band's life at that time." Izzy is seen here at Madison Square Garden's Felt Forum on May 9, 1988.

credit for 'It's So Easy,' as he does on a few *Use Your Illusion* tracks. West's and Duff's initial idea for the song was as an acoustic number, with the lyric sentiment revolving around the idea that the band had no money but it was nonetheless pretty easy living off of girlfriends. The track was the album's first single but by no means its biggest. It was also the subject of a video, a simple live affair, with the band miming in front of a crowd at one of their favorite haunts, the Cathouse. Helping give the album legs, the video didn't arrive until October 1989.

"**Nightrain**" perpetuates the record's sometimes oblique punk vibe, its grime, but applied to old-school boogie rock of an almost Stonesy bent. "'Nightrain' we wrote on acoustic guitars in Izzy's apartment one night before we went out flyering for a gig," recalls Duff. "So we were all drunk on Night Train and walking around the streets postering and singing the chorus to 'Nightrain'—that song really wrote itself." Night Train Express is a low-budget fortified wine favored by poor rockers for the cheap buzz it provides. The track, originated by Slash and Izzy and finished by Duff and Izzy, was issued as a single, rising to #93 on the Billboard charts.

More crunching, grim, and gritty metal (groovy, happy chorus notwithstanding) is afoot with the malevolent "**Out ta Get Me.**" Explains McKagan: "'Out ta Get Me' was, you know, cops breaking into our place. We had this little place and cops broke in. We were like these slovenly gutter rats in Hollywood that the cops were always keeping their eye on. We were not . . . yeah, we were so not part of the hair metal scene. Maybe we were lumped into it way after the fact, but we weren't then. We were considered a punk rock band at the beginning in the club days. We played with Social Distortion and Tex & the Horseheads and Fear and Dickies and Red Hot Chili Peppers. . . . like, we weren't put on bills with Poison or Ruby Slippers or whatever bands."

The ode to heroin "**Mr. Brownstone**" is one of the album's half dozen or so bona fide radio staples, its circular, resolving riff in possession of some of the pixie dust that makes "Welcome to the Jungle" and stripper classic "Paradise City" both so seductive of hook. Axl lays another actorly persona on us, turning in a sort of lounge lizard vocal—or maybe even lizard without the lounge . . . just plain ol' reptilian.

"Izzy came up with the main riff," explains Duff, "and, yes, it's a song about heroin. And it was really prevalent within the collective band's life at that time. Once we got our record advance, before we made the record, we all of a sudden found ourselves with money. It wasn't a lot of money, but to us then it was. It allowed you to exercise your drug habits and stuff [*laughs*]. But it came time for us to do the record and get serious. And Slash and Izzy were both strung out at that point. So they got off it. They took this stuff—I forget the name of it—but it puts you through a three-day withdrawal in one day. And you get incredibly sick and stuff. So I think the words, or the idea for the words, came after this withdrawal."

As the story goes, "Mr. Brownstone" was the first song the guys wrote together after getting signed. The first version of the lyric was put together by Slash and Izzy on a scrap of grocery bag and then brought to Axl for polishing.

"**Paradise City**" is arguably the third most famed track on *Appetite*, following "Sweet Child o' Mine" and "Welcome to the Jungle." Onetime Guns N' Roses guitarist Tracii Guns puts himself into the story. "Me and Izzy were sitting around one day and we were listening to something off of Black Sabbath's *Born*

Again called 'Zero the Hero,'" Guns recalls. "And he just goes, 'Dude, that's a great riff' [*sings the riff*]. Because I never did that song when I was in the band. I had kind of finished up." To his credit, Tracii denies the rumor back in the day that he had written "Paradise City" by himself or that he was paid $20,000 for his efforts.

Slash somewhat supports the connection to "Zero the Hero," telling me, "Actually, in a way, yeah. It was one of those things where I thought 'Zero the Hero' was a great song when it first came out. And I think, in the back of my mind, that was the kind of stuff you pick up, certain stuff like the riff in 'Back in the Saddle' or 'The Ocean' from Zeppelin or something [*laughs*]. That riff had always sort of stuck out for me, and I remember when we first started writing that song, that sort of repetitive chromatic thing came into it naturally. But that's the only part that's the same. The other notes are a little different, and it's also a lot faster. But it does remind me of 'Zero the Hero.'"

Adds Duff, "I'd written the chorus for that one night when I moved to LA, so it was before the band. I was living in this shithole. In 1984, after the Olympics, all the police had basically left Hollywood and it turned into this cesspool. The police and the city had come in and cleaned it up for the Summer Olympics and once that was over, they just left. And for a while, it was just kind of a shithole. It's come back now, like every place has. You can walk through downtown Detroit now without a problem, whereas ten years ago or maybe more, you wouldn't have walked in certain places. So I lived in this apartment and 'Paradise City' was written about an imaginary place that I wasn't in at that point."

"Paradise City" is the only track on the album to feature synthesizer, played by Axl. It's also known for its double-time rave-up at the end. The track vaulted to #5 on the *Billboard* charts when released, again, quite belatedly, in January 1989, backed by "Move to the City" in the US and "Used to Love Her" in the UK, both non-LP cuts. In the video, look for a cameo by Hanoi Rocks guitarist Nasty Suicide.

"**My Michelle**" kicks off side two of the original vinyl, yet another big, gnarly rock monster, Axl sounding angry above an angry soundtrack, the band speeding up into punk mode and then stepping back to the heaviest sort of Aerosmith imaginable, circa "Rats in the Cellar" or "Nobody's Fault." The track's aggression demonstrates Mike Clink's volatile production job, putting in eighteen-hour days for a month with Slash and Axl after working with Steven and Duff for two weeks on the basic tracks.

Says Duff: "Clink was great because we had gotten the record deal and it was time to get a producer. All kinds of different people, like Paul Stanley from Kiss, wanted to do the record. But he wanted Steven to add all these drums and wanted to change the songs and we were like 'Fuck that,' you know? And there was another guy, Spencer Proffer, that big drum sound. We had gone in and done some demos with him. You know, he was a nice guy, but he put Steven on a click track, number one, and we did 'Nightrain,' I think, and it sounded so sterile. It didn't sound like us at all, with his big drum sound and all at crap.

"And finally Clink came down to our rehearsals, and he was a guy who had engineered a couple of Triumph records and nobody had heard of Mike Clink. But he came down and recorded us on his eight-track and it sounded killer! He didn't try to change the songs; he didn't try to do anything. And he says, 'Well, it sounds good. Do you want your record to sound anything like this?' And he just played us back. 'Okay, perfect.'"

Duff, seen here in Middletown, New York, in August 1988, explains that his friend West Arkeen taught him the open-E tuning used to write the first single, "It's So Easy."

Steven Adler stresses the importance of hydration in 1988. Duff recalls how early attempts to make Steven play to a click track in the studio sounded "sterile."

"My Michelle" was written for a friend of the band named Michelle Young, who is thanked in the liner notes. Axl says that he was with Young in a car when Elton John's "Your Song" came on the radio, with Michelle remarking that it would be nice if someone wrote a song about her one day. As the song progressed, it became a squalid tale of drug addiction and harsh family life, but Axl presented it to her and she approved of the message despite how she was painted.

Cowbell-banged party rock 'n' roller **"Think About You"** was written primarily by Izzy and is one of the album's lesser-known tracks. Somewhat of an inconsequential rocker (distinguishing feature: an acoustic guitar overdub as texture), this one is followed by the up-tempo ballad **"Sweet Child o' Mine."** As Tracii Guns recalls, "I believe it was Nikki Sixx that told me this story, that Slash had told him they were in a motorhome on the way back from a gig up north and they were just fucking around with it. I remember even when we were in junior high school, Slash had this guitar teacher, and he used to always come up with these high riffs, chicken-scratch riffs. So when I first heard 'Sweet Child o' Mine,' I thought that's where that came from. It's a great song. Bought those guys mansions and drugs and cars and hookers."

"Tracii wouldn't know where the fuck that came from," laughs Slash. "No, it was just something I made up while I was sitting around with Izzy. And it's not an exercise, but it's just one of those quirky little things I do when I'm fucking around. It just happened to be something I stumbled on that afternoon. So I was more just trying to perfect it, because it was a little more left field; it's not a predictable style [*laughs*] or guitar player kind of note configuration or whatever. So once I stumbled on it, I was just trying to perfect it. Izzy started playing the chords that went underneath it, and I sort of transposed a couple of notes to fit the chords. And then Axl heard us doing it, and all of a sudden he was onto something. And I hated that song [*laughs*]. But it had nothing to do with any guitar teachers at all."

"That's written about Axl's girlfriend at the time, ex-wife later, Erin," adds Duff, referring to Erin Everly, daughter of Don Everly. The couple had been together since 1986, married in 1990, and done by the end of the year. "I'll tell you something about that song. We wrote the song really as a joke. Axl was serious about the lyrics, but we were like, 'Fuucck—a ballad?! Come on.' So you know, that beginning guitar riff? It was absolutely written as a joke, at first. It was meant to sound funny. If you listen to it, it's goofy. But like everything at that point for us, it worked [*laughs*]. Everything worked. But it was really written as a goofy . . . like a circus riff, because nobody wanted to do this thing."

Slash agrees that there was a "no ballads" sentiment rifling through the band. "Yes, and especially in the early days, or at that particular point in Guns N' Roses' career, fuckin' we were so hard-edged that ballads just seemed so sappy. . . . I used to dread having to walk out to the front of the stage and start playing that lick. And for the longest time, I couldn't always play it right [*laughs*]. Like I say, it's not the most conventional finger styling."

"Sweet Child o' Mine" zoomed to #1 on the *Billboard* charts, helped on its trajectory by an iconic video featuring Rose's distinctive slinky dance moves. Also in the video are the GN'R crew and all the guys' girlfriends at the time as well as Izzy's dog. As part of the slowly evolving story of the album's success, this very obvious single wasn't issued as such until eleven months after the album proper had hit the shops. The UK would wait a further two months, with the song reaching #24, and then #6 upon rerelease in May 1989. The single version of the song loses about a minute of guitar jamming.

Duff says "Sweet Child o' Mine" saved the album, given that through '87 it had been doing okay but not setting any sales records. "Oh yeah, man . . . we were out touring, I think, for ten months, and Eddie Rosenblatt and David Geffen told Tom [Zutaut] to pull us off the road, that they were done sending us tour support. And then 'Sweet Child' came out, the softest song on the record, and that's the thing that crossed us over. It made the rest of that record palatable, and then there was a sort of undercurrent of a huge swath of youth that could identify with songs like 'It's So Easy.'"

After the success of the record's "power ballad," one wonders if there had been pressure from Geffen for more of that, to become more of a conventional hair metal band, as it were.

"Oh no, we would have never done that," Duff continues. "We would have never, ever done that. We would have disbanded the band before we did that. We didn't care about business. If we cared about business, we would have made a lot of other moves. If we cared about just making a quick buck, we would have sold our publishing for $250,000 when it was offered to us back in 1986, you know? That's quick and easy money, right? So we just kind of believed in ourselves and our music."

"You're Crazy" is arguably the heaviest, most frantic and frightful track on the album, followed by the tough, street-embattled, funky Aerosmith metal of **"Anything Goes"** and another groovy manifestation of Aerosmith funk gone punk, **"Rocket Queen."** "Anything Goes" is one of the band's oldest songs, originating as a 1981 composition called "My Way, Your Way." As for "Rocket Queen," Axl said it was written about a gal called Barbi Von Greif who said she was going to form a band called Rocket Queen, fly into outer space, and play concerts on various planets en route to ruling the universe. As for the music, Slash notes that he and Duff had originally put that song together back in their Road Crew days. "Rocket Queen" is also notorious for the recorded moans of Adiana Smith, who had been recorded having sex with Axl in the vocal booth at Mediasound Studios during the mixing sessions for the album.

"I mean, *Appetite* is *Appetite*," laughs Slash. "That's like a signature stamp of a band in a period or in a place, where we were at. And it's really . . . it's pretty inimitable. It is what it is, in that we're the only guys who could have done it. It was at that time, and we were all really young and it's got a certain kind of raw aggression to it. I don't think the playing is really all that proficient on it, but it's got a certain kind of fucking aggressive, in-your-face sonic thing to it. So I'm a fan of it, although probably not the way that other people are. It's just something that when I hear it, it sounds cool and everything is in its place. Mistakes and all, it sounds good."

10
NOVEMBER RAIN

GN'R issues *GN'R Lies*

This still from the "It's So Easy" video was shot at the infamous Cathouse in Los Angeles on October 10, 1989. The occasion was also framed as a warm-up gig for the band's opening slot with the Rolling Stones a week later.

Back in LA after dates with Alice Cooper, the pressure was on for Guns N' Roses to begin work on a second record. But there was also more hard living and touring to do, so instead the guys tumbled into Rumbo Recorders and recorded a number of acoustic songs with the idea of getting a second EP out. With Mike Clink presiding once again, a bunch of drunks made their way through new originals "Patience," "Used to Love Her," and "One in a Million," along with a laid-back remake of "You're Crazy" and a profane anal sex song called "Cornshucker," sung by Duff and smartly destined for the cutting room floor.

The songs saw the light of day after much more life at a million miles an hour, when on November 30, 1988, *GN'R Lies* was issued, with the acoustic songs on side two and the four *Live ?!*@ Like a Suicide* songs stuck on side two, making the now $100 collectible EP available to the masses. To those who liked their discographies tidy, Guns N' Roses were flipping the bird and living up to their reputation for chaos. And they knew as much, going with a sort of *National Enquirer* front cover, and no clear idea of a title, with the original idea being something like *Lies! The Sex, The Drugs, The Violence, The Shocking Truth*. Plus, half of it was previously released but not really, independently but not really, and they're even covering themselves with the new "You're Crazy." And at thirty-three minutes, many agreed that *GN'R Lies* was an LP and not an EP, and it was tabulated on the charts and sales-wise in that light. To add messiness, it didn't count as an album toward the band's contract with Geffen, so initial promotion was scant accordingly. To add further messiness, given the faked live concept of the EP, *GN'R Lies* was called a studio album.

As this perplexing bit of product hit the street, "Welcome to the Jungle" had climbed to #14 on the Billboard charts and *Appetite for Destruction* had just been certified an astounding four-times-platinum. The band also had just appeared on the cover of *Rolling Stone*, as legend has it, in place of Aerosmith, whom the magazine visited for interviews on the GN'R/Aerosmith tour, perceptively

This and following page: The Felt Forum, Madison Square Garden, New York City, May 9, 1988

Axl and band perform
at New York City's Felt
Forum, May 9, 1988. The
last four tracks on *Lies*
were acoustic numbers that
the band recorded in '88.

Opposite: UIC Pavilion,
Chicago, August 21, 1987.
Alice Cooper worries that
his bodybuilding guitarist
Kane Roberts (back row,
second from right) is going
to crush the life out of
every last member of the
biggest-selling rock band
on the planet.

changing their mind midstream. The November 17, 1988, issue, #539, declared the band "HARD-ROCK HEROES," sticking them on a stark white background like Kiss on the *Lick It Up* cover. Within a week of release, *Appetite* was certified six-times-platinum. As *GN'R Lies* vaulted to #2 in the Billboard charts in February 1989 (its top posting), the Gunners established themselves as the only band in the '80s to have two albums in the top five at the same time.

As for the contents, Axl was never happy with his vocals, citing fatigue from touring. But he loved the music, and why not? This was the band showing a different dimension, and actually a classic rock one, presaging and predicting the whole *MTV Unplugged* thing—but first Tesla—while evoking memories of the Stones and Led Zeppelin, and also tapping into the mushy fan base that appreciated "Sweet Child o' Mine."

Side two opens with "Patience," which turned out to be the big hit of the album, issued as a single on April 8, 1989. It's now the most famous song ever with whistling, and it rocketed to #4 on the Billboard charts. It's a sad love song, involved at nearly six minutes, and is assumed to be about Axl's troubled relationship with his then-wife, Erin Everly. Recorded with three acoustic guitars, the only member not accounted for is Steven Adler, although he appears in the iconic arch-hair metal video, as does producer Mike Clink.

Next is "Used to Love Her," a song with a shocking murder lyric, although Izzy's idea was more of a joke, having heard a Great White song on the radio that he thought was overly maudlin. He called it a "real New York–type song." The credit on it goes to the whole band, and it's understood that Axl and Duff came up with the lyrics. It had been played live back to the previous year, and moving forward, both Axl and Slash made sure to say that the song was meant as a goof, and that the band didn't condone wife-beating.

Talk about goofy, "You're Crazy" is delivered in a sort of twangy, funky bluegrass arrangement, not far off "Used to Love Her," which sounds like Creedence Clearwater–styled country music. Essentially the messaging is that of Van Halen's "Happy Trails" from *Diver Down*, or "Could This Be Magic? from *Women and Children First*, the idea that Guns N' Roses could get away with this because they're part of a grand tradition reaching back past Jimmy Page to Woody Guthrie as well as the blues.

The whistling is back for our final selection, "One in a Million," but of course everybody remembers Axl's shocking lyrics, where he rails against immigrants, blacks, and homosexuals, before executing a curious backpedal, where he calls out "radicals and racists." As Axl has framed it, it's about getting hustled at the Greyhound bus station upon his storied arrival in LA from Indiana. He's also spoken about previous instances getting propositioned hitchhiking and getting robbed. The song caused issues moving forward, adding to the narrative that Guns N' Roses served as a lightning rod for chaos wherever they went. In fact, anticipating controversy, the very cover art of *GN'R Lies* included an apology for the song.

In any event, *GN'R Lies* reached five-times-platinum, again, driven to those sales numbers, at the underbelly, by the subversive "Used to Love Her" and "One in a Million," but in the main by "Patience," which was like an intravenous delivery of all the things the guys found wimpy about "Sweet Child o' Mine." Of course, it was also driven to those numbers by the meteoric success of *Appetite for Destruction*. And given its half-archival reality, it's essentially *Dirty Deeds Done Dirt Cheap* ushered out in 1981 after *Back in Black*, a plundering of the vaults to capitalize on Geffen suddenly being dealt the hottest of hands.

11
SHOTGUN BLUES
Opening for the Rolling Stones

Mick Jagger and Axl pose
for a picture on stage
during the Stones' *Steel
Wheels* tour, late 1989,
while Izzy drinks it all in.

Opening for the Rolling Stones is an anointing, and it happened
for the likes of ZZ Top, Lynyrd Skynyrd, Santana, and Prince,
and now the Stones wanted Guns N' Roses. The *Steel Wheels* tour
also was touting Living Colour as the next big thing, but bigger
than everybody was the Stones stage show, supersized for the
well-received *Steel Wheels* album. Although it was the event of the
year, with the most excitement and goodwill thrown the band's
way since *Tattoo You*, selling out four shows at a stadium was an
enormous ask, even for the Stones.

Appetite for Destruction was now eight-times-platinum,
although the album's last single, "Nightrain," was fizzling.
Slash was a mess as was Izzy, who was arrested at the Phoenix
airport for smoking in the nonsmoking section on his flight, plus
haranguing a stewardess and urinating on the floor of the plane,

incensed that he had to wait for the bathroom. All the while he was trying to get clean and Axl was getting fed up. *GN'R Lies* then is certified triple platinum and "Sweet Child o' Mine" wins at the MTV awards show, with both Izzy and Axl jamming with Tom Petty—Axl had already jumped onstage with Petty the previous month in Syracuse, singing "Free Fallin'" and "Knockin' on Heaven's Door." Backstage, Vince Neil sucker punches Izzy in the face, cutting him with his ring. Relations were better with Hanoi Rocks' influential frontman Michael Monroe, who jams with the band at a *RIP* magazine party. The gig is taken on board to see if the guys could function onstage, having not played at this point for eight months. Apparently, they couldn't, with Axl telling the guys he was quitting the band.

In the couple of months leading up to the proposed generational showdown, manager Alan Niven, against the band's wishes, declined the Stones' offer of $50,000 a show, for four opening slots at the Los Angeles Memorial Coliseum. The offer is raised to $500,000 for the complete run, with Niven asking for, and securing, a cool $1 million. As it turned out, the payout was justified because a large portion of the ticket sales was attributed to Guns N' Roses being in the bill.

The guys were excited about the shows, despite Keith Richards being dismissive of the band, particularly their look. Axl was gracious, saying that the Stones were among the band's many influences, perceptively adding that the Stones taught them that they could do anything they want with their music—once the *Use Your Illusion* albums arrived, the sort of creative parallels with the Stones would become more pronounced. Slash wasn't put off by Richards's words either, shrugging that if they got to know the Guns N' Roses better, they'd probably like them.

On October 18, 1989, just five days after the *RIP* party at the Parkview Plaza Hotel, the band gathered to hit the stage in advance of Jagger and Richards. Axl was a no-show, and what ensues was typically surreal for this band: management had to send the LAPD out to hunt him down and essentially arrest him and get him to the gig. Everything was ready by 8 p.m., and the band got a typically hyped introduction.

But there's no music. Responding to Vernon Reid from Living Colour calling out "One in a Million," Axl goes into a long expletive-filled rant about the song's lyrics, half explaining himself but also half doubling down, pretty much blowing up the problem even worse in front of seventy thousand fans. They get through a ragged "It's So Easy," but right away, there's more. "I hate to do this onstage," began Axl, figuring he hadn't done enough damage with his first rant. "But I tried every other fucking way. And unless certain people in this band get their shit together, these will be the last Guns N' Roses shows you'll fucking ever see. 'Cause I'm tired of too many people in this organization dancing with Mr. god-damn Brownstone."

Left to right: Axl Rose, Charlie Watts, Keith Richards, Mick Jagger, Duff McKagan, Izzy Stradlin, and Steven Adler on the Rolling Stones' *Steel Wheels* tour in Los Angeles, 1989

The band rumble into "Mr. Brownstone" (bum notes included), but then by the night's third selection, "Out ta Get Me," Axl strides right off the stage into space and falls into the photographer's pit. Fortunately, he doesn't miss a beat, and both the song and the set continues. What feels like an agonizing lifetime later, Slash memorably blows the solo in "Sweet Child o' Mine."

Throughout the set, the band are fighting each other, and the timing is a mess and there are more bum notes. Axl manages to sound hostile with his vocals as well, lapsing into the conversational and getting casual with his phrasing. But it's not a surprise. Axl had planted it in the guys' heads that the partnership was over. After Axl's hurtful and very public words, Duff recalls shrinking with embarrassment and Slash recalls his hatred for Axl growing, sure that Axl was referring to him specifically. Generally speaking, there was the thought that some sort of gang code had been broken through such a public airing of the band's internal strife. In case anybody didn't get the message, up into the "Paradise City" encore, Axl hit the hot mic again, saying, "I'd like to announce this is my last gig with Guns N' Roses and this is called 'Paradise City' because there ain't no fucking place anywhere." Later that night, Mick Jagger quipped from the stage, "I think Axl did a good show, but I wish he'd just shut up and play."

Relations didn't improve much on the following night. Axl had in fact said he wasn't showing up for any more of the gigs unless Slash made an announcement from the stage acknowledging the band's issues with drugs, which he dutifully did, at much length, suitably over the intro to "Mr. Brownstone." By the third show, after a day off, Slash was describing the band's performance as "magic." The fourth and final show took place as planned on the 22nd, so all told, it was a remarkable recovery. Still, band relations were irreparably harmed, and one by one, acrimony mixed with drugs knocked everybody out of the band except for our beloved Dennis the Menace at the mic.

The GN'R guitar team in 1988—closer in temperament and writing style than one would think, given their diverging futures

12
RECKLESS LIFE
Farm Aid IV, Steven's last show with the band

It seems logical, but when a bunch of drug addicts try to fire a fellow drug addict (and good friend) from the band, through the darkness they can sympathize. Plus, this was Steven Adler, who the guys relied upon since the beginning as the magic push-and-pull of the band's sound. The good news is that Slash was getting better, and Duff was functional too. So, there was a songwriting core of the band moving forward, coming up with songs, making plans, showing up at awards shows to haul away trophies.

In fact, the band convened at Rumbo Recorders and got through about eighteen songs with Steven, or despite Steven, really, who had been nodding out at the kit due to his heavy heroin use, plus using crack and lying to the guys about all of it. There was the February 12, 1990, call from manager Doug Goldstein on the night of a Mötley Crüe show Steven was all excited about attending, informing Steven that he'd been fired—Steven promptly disappeared into the bathroom and didn't emerge for hours. But that call was more of a scare job. The band also let Steven know they were auditioning drummers, like Fred Coury from Cinderella, Adam Maples from Seahags, and Martin Chambers from the Pretenders, but their hearts weren't in it, and they quietly hoped it would shock Steven into getting help. Duff also threatened Steven's drug dealer with a gun and the contract, signed by Steven on March 28, where he gave up partnership in the band. However, the door was open through a thirty-day probationary period, whereby if he could kick drugs, all might be forgiven. There was talk that Goldstein even dangled an appearance with the band at Rock in Rio up into January 1991 in front of Steven, in hopes that forecasting well into the future might help him focus.

The last song Steven recorded for the band was "Civil War." Considered one of Guns N' Roses' most ambitious and mature songs, the track was issued on the *Nobody's Child: Romanian Angel Appeal* charity album, issued July 23, 1990. As Steven explains it, trying to beat heroin cold turkey and significantly dopesick, his doctor had put him on an opiate blocker, which just made him

sicker. This coincided with the "Civil War" sessions scheduled for three days later, which could only have been postponed at great cost. During the recording, Steven could barely function through the pain in his bones, lurching his way through his backing tracks twenty or thirty times, according to Steven himself. The final version is a massive edit job and even a percussive collaboration, not that fans would notice. Of note, it is also the first track to feature newly hired keyboardist Dizzy Reed.

The track came in handy, serving as an advance single and then getting put proudly as the first song on *Use Your Illusion II*, despite its length, tempo, and quasi-ballad structure. It's Steven's only performance on the album, although there are indeed several demos that have circulated, which, incidentally, sound solid, even if you'd have to be a drummer to distinguish the performance as particularly better or different from what Matt Sorum accomplished.

"Civil War" also figured into Steven's last performance with Guns N' Roses. On April 7, 1990, the band took part in Farm Aid IV, at the Hoosier Dome in Indianapolis, playing just that song—for the first time ever—and a cover of the UK Subs' "Down on the Farm." Steven bounced onto the stage and tripped into his drum riser, signaling to the guys that he was well N' high. Steven claims the guys had kept him in the dark as to what songs they were going to even play that night, as if to sabotage him further. The truth seems to be that he knew they were going to do "Civil War," but he was completely surprised by "Down on the Farm," which he'd never heard in his life, hence the story of Duff quickly clapping out the beat for him.

But it's also believed then even risking bringing Steven to Farm Aid just might have been enough to get him to change his ways. As for his performance, he pulls off "Down in the Farm" well, pushing the song powerfully and adding more interesting fills than the UK Subs ever did. "Civil War," on the other hand, is played uneasily slow, which often happens with a drummer on smack. Still, Steven keeps it strong and steady, making this last performance of his something to remember, an uncommonly doomy and yet muscular version of this impactful classic.

In any event, the band's patience, after five intensely hard-living years for everybody, had run out, with Steven's firing finally sticking on July 11, 1990, although the news was kept quiet. Two months later, on September 6, an MTV interview aired with Axl telling the world, "Steven didn't quit the band. Steven was fired. We gave him every ultimatum. We tried working with other drummers. We had Steven sign a contract saying if he went back to drugs, then he was out. He couldn't leave his drugs."

Steven sued the band, the crux of it being that his performance on the studio version of "Civil War" was compromised because he was trying to get clean, and that the band owed him some extra degree of patience. He actually settled, receiving $2.25 million in compensation, but of course, that wasn't going to help get him back in the band. For his part, Izzy Stradlin left the band a year later and he regrets that they didn't do more for Steven, purely for the sake of the band, essentially saying that Guns N' Roses never sounded that good ever again.

Given the band's lifestyle, it seemed only a matter of time before someone couldn't cut it. Drummer Steven Adler was the first member left by the wayside.

Guns N' Roses at Farm Aid IV, Hoosier Dome, Indianapolis, Indiana, April 7, 1990

13
OUT TA GET ME
"Knockin' on Heaven's Door" features Matt Sorum's GN'R debut

"We couldn't just put an ad in the paper," quipped Slash, on the predicament the band was in after deciding that Steven wasn't coming back. But he and Duff had toured with the Cult, had caught the band recently, in July 1989, and were now, on April 3, 1990, catching the band's last show of their current tour at the Universal Amphitheatre in support of the hit album *Sonic Temple*, issued exactly a year previous. Slash was hesitant to even go to the show, having planned a date with the woman who is now his wife, but he turned it into a concert date, and then a work date of sorts, studying the drummer from the soundboard. Matt Sorum also came with a recommendation from Metallica's Lars Ulrich.

It is said that right then and there, Duff and Slash decided Matt would do the trick, but then reports conflict about how it all went down, complicated by the idea that Matt would record the *Use Your Illusion* tracks, but that Steven might return for the tour. There also was the possibility that Matt had been borrowed, and that he would return to the Cult when needed. In any event, the guys got down to work and loved Matt's solid sense of time, the fact that he hit hard, and that he likely was more suited to the band's adventurous and sometimes technical new material, thinking Steven might have been too traditional to pull off these new songs anyway. Additionally, it seems like Matt was a good influence, keeping everybody in line (Axl's exact words) to the point of Matt even saying, "It was hell in the band, and I patched things up." In short, his personality was agreeable; he was always in a good mood, friendly, and efficient. As Axl puts it, the guys managed to do twenty-nine tracks in a month, and you get the feeling that Matt was a big part of making that happen.

Matt, thirty, was born in Long Beach, California, and had been a surfer through tenth grade and a drug smuggler. He'd played in bands around town for years, including Gladys Knight and the Pips, Belinda Carlisle, and Tori Amos, as part of Y Kant Tori Read. His first concert was Kiss, back in 1975, and he'd been hooked on hard rock ever since, plus fusion. The Cult seemed more aligned with Matt's soul, finally, after much toil. But not much more. It's almost like these post-punk Brits were meeting the surfer halfway. Not like it was ever realized on record, because Matt's not on any of them, not on *Electric* or *Sonic Temple*. Maybe he represents what a Hollyrock version of the Cult might have been, perhaps something intriguingly Guns N' Roses–adjacent. And then he was gone.

The first collaboration between Matt and GN'R was a studio rendition of the band's often-played Bob Dylan cover, "Knockin' on Heaven's Door." The song was issued on the gold-certified *Days of Thunder* soundtrack album on June 26, 1990, fourteen months before its appearance on *Use Your Illusion* (slightly modified) and one month before "Civil War," which features the band's old drummer, Steven. It was a moderate hit at the time, and then more of a hit when the two *Use Your Illusion* albums flooded the world with new Guns N' Roses songs. Perhaps most saliently, it became a classic rock radio staple over time, pervasive without the hard stats. And like "Civil War," with both songs long and slow, "Knockin' at Heaven's Door" raised Guns N' Roses from the top of some imagined dirty hair metal heap into the pantheon of the greats. I mean, there was always authenticity there, but these two isolated, reflective, pensive songs lent the band gravitas as well, coming from a band for which gravitas was something only occasionally chased and embraced.

It's funny, but "Knockin' on Heaven's Door" and "Civil War" served the same purpose as playing with the Stones. Essentially, in lieu of a new album, here's Guns N' Roses functioning, participating in the world or at least the music business. Plus, it was a classic rock cover, linking the band to decades of rock history. Even though it seems like it was a huge hit in North America, it meant even more around the world, topping the charts in Ireland, Belgium, the Netherlands, and Portugal, and reaching #2 in the UK, where it also certified as a gold single.

As it turns out, Matt's first show with the band was January 20, 1991, at the intense and immense Rock in Rio date dangled in front of Steven Adler to get him clean. Matt recalls it as even more surreal than one might imagine. First, it's a stadium that fits 140,000 people, and second, he never once rehearsed with Axl. Plus, it was going to be recorded for television and there was basically no setlist. On the first night, the band opened with a

new song called "Pretty Tied Up," which counts off with high hat.
There were two nights in total, and then that would be it for four
months, over and done—what just happened?

What happened was that Matt was not going back to the Cult.
Basically, he had been in negotiations with Ian and Bily to become
a full-fledged, equal member of the band, and that wasn't really
going anywhere, so he thought he'd ask the same of Guns N'
Roses to seal the deal and they said yes. The switchover had been
fully amicable anyway, with Duff and Slash clearing it with Ian
and Billy, who were working on the idea of making the Cult all-
British again anyway.

ACT THREE
INSANITY

14
BREAKDOWN
Axl Rose leaves midshow in St. Louis, causing a riot

In Philadelphia, two weeks before the *Use Your Illusion* juggernaut rolled into the Riverport Amphitheatre in St. Louis, Axl already had witnessed a skirmish between a fan and band photographer Robert John and challenged the fan to a fight. Now the guys were playing in a shed just two weeks old in the Maryland Heights area north of St. Louis, having just jammed a guitar solo, a drum solo, and their brief ensemble instrumental version of the "Love Theme from *The Godfather*."

At this point, capable openers Skid Row had finished, it was about 11:15 p.m., and the Gunners had played for about ninety minutes. They were about a dozen songs in with a half dozen to go. What's cool is that the *Use Your Illusion* albums were still two months away, and yet they performed eight of the forthcoming songs. But they make their way into the first chorus of "Rocket Queen" when Axl, resplendent in shorts, no shirt, half-length fur coat, big cross around his neck, and a miliary cap hiding his eyes, points into the crowd. There's someone with a camera taking pictures, which, before the near total penetration of cellphone ownership, was generally not allowed. Axl lowers his voice and says, quite calmly, "Hey, take that, take that. Now, get that guy and take that." Before anybody can react, he says, "I'll take it; goddamn it!" and he removes his cap and hurls himself horizontally into the front row.

Amusingly, the band keep playing that sweet "Rocket Queen" riff, first regular and then pianissimo as Axl finds himself in the pit. The guy taking pictures, "Stump," was part of a local biker gang called the Saddle Tramps. At a previous show, he had taken shots of Axl without incident, later explaining that Axl had even acknowledged him and threw him a few shapes. So, Axl confronts Stump, leaps from the extended catwalk, and lands on him. As it turns out, Stump had fallen back and ruptured a disc in his back when he landed on some chairs. Eventually, he'd have to be taken off on a stretcher, the route being right over the top of the stage and out the back.

After thirty seconds of being in the pit, as well as landing a punch on one of the security detail, Axl is gathered up and stuck back onstage, fur coat intact, where a brave roadie hands him his microphone. Additionally ticked off because he'd lost a contact lens in the fight, without missing a beat, he says, "Well, thanks to the lame-ass security, I'm going home!," after which he slams down the mic and storms off. Slash responds with, "He smashed the microphone; we're outta here."

There was a chance that the band would return and finish the show, but before that could happen, the lights came on and the "get out of the venue" music started playing through the PA. The crowd begins hurling stuff at the stage, and one of the Gunners' roadies takes offense and responds with a rude gesture, taunting the crowd. A riot ensues. The police rapidly arrive, ringing the stage, and immediately find themselves in a confrontation, swinging batons amidst a mob hollering "Fuck you, pigs!" A ripped-up seat sailed through the air onto the stage, striking a security guard in the head, requiring a trip to the hospital for thirty or forty stitches.

Busted, and not for the first time

The last line of defense fell when authorities rolled a firehose out onstage, but there was no water pressure. At this point, the cops retreated, and the riot intensified, tallying more than sixty-five injuries to fans and twenty-five to police officers, along with dozens of arrests. Hundreds of thousands of dollars of damage was incurred at the concert hall, including the video screens, various lighting, and sound equipment and even the newly planted trees at the freshly landscaped outdoor space, with newly planted turf being torn up and set on fire. Fans were swinging from cables in the lighting rig, which swayed back and forth precariously, but, in the end, it held, averting what could have been numerous deaths. Band equipment that wasn't trashed was stolen, including mixing equipment and heavy amps that were calmly wheeled out the doors, where battles between the cops and fans continued and more of the injured were attended to.

For his part, Axl reiterated after the fact that the security was indeed ineffectual on that night, not enforcing drinking rules and even allowing firearms into the venue. He said they ignored requests from the band's security detail about photography, and that while performing, they had been hit with bottles.

A couple of dates were canceled before the guys could put their show back together again, in time for Dallas on July 8. On that night though, by the time the legal system could respond, the band had been whisked out of the state, to Illinois. It wasn't until July 12 the following year that Axl was arrested, at JFK Airport in New York, and charged with inciting a riot. Held for ten hours, he promised he would appear for trial in St. Louis later in the week. Ultimately, only a year later, it was ruled that Axl wasn't directly responsible for the riot, but he was found guilty of assault and property damage. He was given two years probation along with having to make a $50,000 donation to a local charity. A special arrangement had to be made with his probation rules so that he could associated with people within his band that had been convicted of crimes. Stump and his testimony were part of the trial, and afterward, as Axl was giving a press conference, Stump walked right up to Axl and asked him to sign his pictures, which, to his credit, he did.

The unfortunate event was memorialized forevermore with a "Fuck you, St. Louis!" missive tucked into the liner notes' thank-you section included as part of the two new albums. Ending a ban on the band in St. Louis, Guns N' Roses returned to the city for the first time since the riot on July 27, 2017, but just in case, they played an indoor venue downtown and not the fated outdoor shed.

Axl sits handcuffed in the back of a police car after he was arrested at Kennedy Airport upon his return from a European concert tour. He was charged with four counts of misdemeanor assault and one count of property damage stemming from a riot during a concert in 1991 in St. Louis, Missouri. Axl pleaded innocent to the charges and was later given two years probation and forced to donate $50,000 to charity.

15
WELCOME TO THE JUNGLE

GN'R issues *Use Your Illusion I*

"I remember when those records came out," reflects Duff. "The night it happened, the record company took Slash and I out to this dinner. You know the Tower Records on Sunset in West Hollywood; they open it up at midnight if a record like that is coming out. And the fucking line went half a mile down Sunset. And they took us to this place behind Tower Records and put us in this office where you could see down and watch the people coming in, through this one-way glass. And we were just watching this thing, these people just waiting in line, going nuts for your record, you know?"

September 17, 1991, was indeed a big day in the lives of the Gunners, with 152 minutes of music released to the masses all at once, on independently issued CDs called *Use Your Illusion I* and *Use Your Illusion II*. There are conflicting stories about whether Axl wanted to issue this music as a double album or not, inspired by Led Zeppelin with *Physical Graffiti*. But whether he had to come around or not, in the end, everybody thought it was cool—and easier on the pocketbooks of the fans—to do something that had never been done before. In any event, here we celebrate the songs on the first one, although Duff cautions us not to apply too much significance with respect to which of the band's murder ballads wound up on *I* versus *II*, or whether there are distinct personas between them.

A detail of Raphael's *The School of Athens*, which appears in adapted form on the covers of the two *Illusion* albums

Opposite: Axl and former girlfriend Gina Siler—rumored to be the inspiration for at least one of the *Use Your Illusion* tracks.

"Well, we all had copies of the songs, and we all had our suggestions on what we thought would flow the best. It was all kind of put together and we took the best ideas. At some point, we just said fine, fuck it, it's the right order. You can spend a long time looking at it, especially with five guys. You know, check it out—those records came out four months into our *Use Your Illusion* tour. So, I never had the time to sit down and listen to one or the other. We were playing the songs and we toured for two-and-a-half years, and the last thing I wanted to do when I got back from that was listen to those records. So, I never actually have. I've never sat down and listened to them and tried to figure out one from the other. I don't think any of us have. If you asked any one of us that question, the answer might be, 'I don't fucking know!'"

And making it tougher to discern, there really doesn't seem to be any rhyme or reason to the sequencing of the collection's thirty tracks. There could have been some obvious organizing, and then we'd all have an opinion about a narrative. But the fact that the albums are, in summation, like each other obscures any strong views. Plus, as Duff says, it's five guys (plus, presumably, colleagues and coworkers, folks at the label), dealing with thirty songs across two albums—the math gets exponential pretty fast.

Unifying them further, the albums share the same cover art, with graphic artist Mark Kostabi's highlighting one figure and recessing the other from a small portion of *The School of Athens*, a painting by Raphael circa 1509 to 1511. Kostabi had titled his adapted piece *Use Your Illusion*, and Axl had spotted it after roaming the local art galleries in hopes of finding a work suitable to use as a cover. Then, of course, the first album is themed red and yellow and the second blue and purple, both named and titled with the distinctive elongated "Edition" font the band first used on *Appetite*. The wax seal on the back might remind one of the fellow ridiculously successful Geffen act Whitesnake, who used a similar device in their graphics. A nice touch is the photo collage included in the booklet, where the band includes shots of their many friends and facilitators.

Use Your Illusion I opens with "Right Next Door to Hell," commemorating Axl's feud with his neighbor Gabriella Kantor. At the music end, it's a co-write with Timo Kaltio from Hanoi Rocks, Finland's proto Guns N' Roses from the early '80s.

Immediately one can hear Mike Clink's tougher, more face-forward production, specifically with the jagged guitars and the exacting drum sounds from Matt Sorum. He's new to the band, and so there's a stylistic difference there too, a sort of merciless violence. Part of Matt's hard-surface sound might have to do with the issues the band had mixing the album. They started the process with Bob Clearmountain and had recorded twenty-one tracks in when the bands caught wind through Clearmountain's notes that he was planning to augment some of Matt's tracks with sampled drums. Subsequently, they handed the job over to Bill Price of Sex Pistols fame. Not like the end result sounds anything like *Never Mind the Bollocks*, but there's a punk excitement and urgency to the sound picture, nonetheless.

From the punky Aerosmith of "Right Next Door to Hell," we transition to the bluesy Aerosmith of "Dust N' Bones." In that sense, with two tracks under our belts, we're essentially carrying on from *Appetite for Destruction* as if four years of mayhem hasn't dented our heads. Izzy Stradlin provides lead vocals on "Dust N' Bones" (with much help from Axl), as well as "You Ain't the First" and "Double Talkin' Jive."

But now the band spread their wings (pun not intended), with a surprising cover of "Live and Let Die." It's a production tour de force, and like the Clash with *London Calling* or U2 with *Rattle and Hum*, it's this band signaling that they want to be part of the universal classic-rock story and not just outlaw Hollyrock. Besides, it's a bit of an in-joke among headbangers that this is the one where Paul McCartney and Wings put together a heavy metal riff. "Live and Let Die" was issued as the album's second single, getting to #33 in the charts and garnering a Grammy nomination. The iconic video for the track marks the last time we'd see Izzy Stradlin as part of the band in a video.

Next is "Don't Cry," a song with a history (Axl has called it the first song they ever wrote together) but nonetheless another departure from *Appetite*, given that it's even less rock 'n' rollsy than "Sweet Child o' Mine." If this is a power ballad, it's a cut above, sophisticated of chord change, triumphant in flashes. The band thought it was so good that they stuck a version on both *Illusion* albums, the second with different verses and a few musical adjustments. To complicate things further, the CD single issue of the song contains

The Sports Palace, Mexico City, April 2, 1992

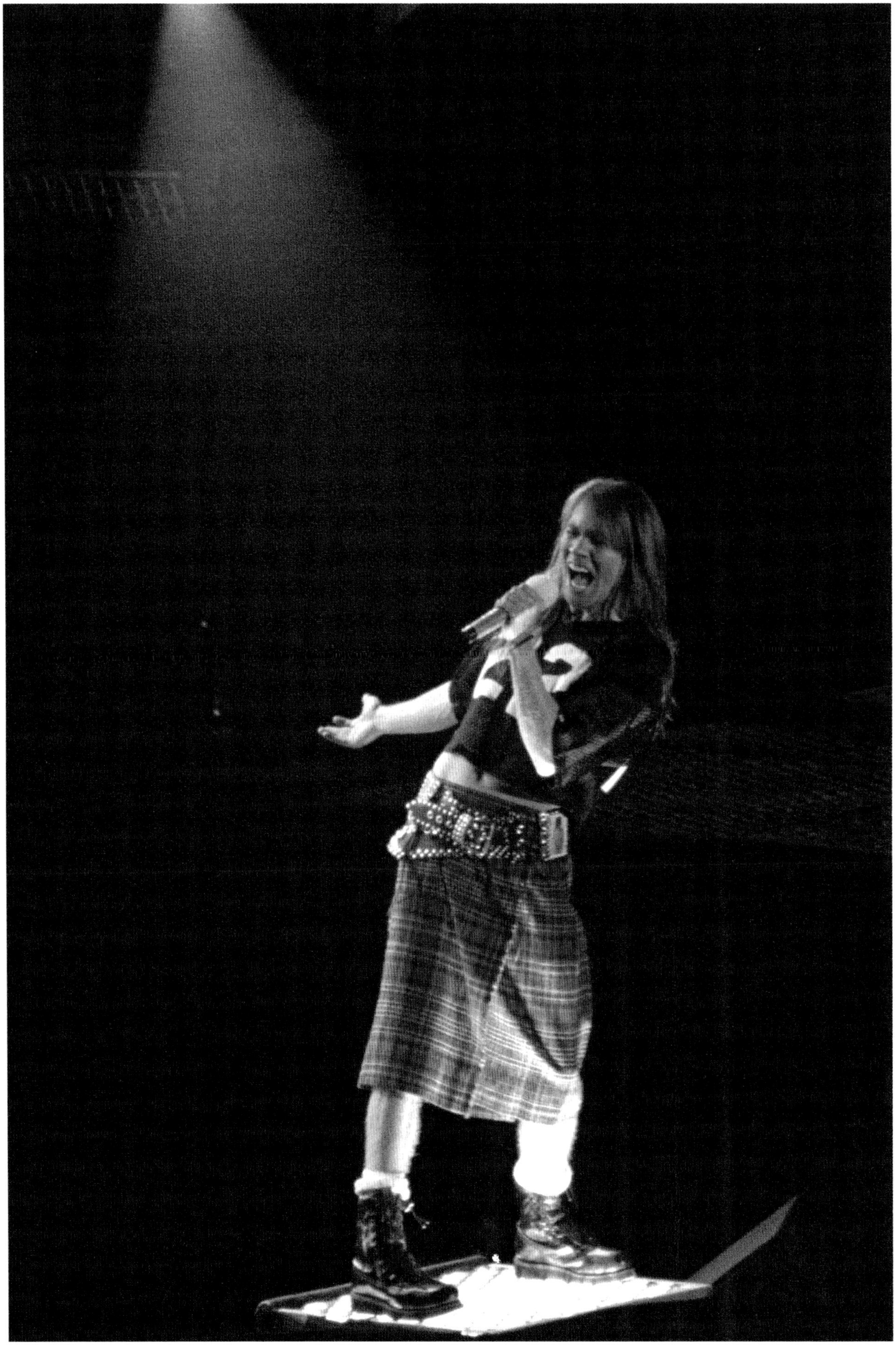

both *Illusion* versions as well as a Mystic Studio Sessions demo version from 1985. The song celebrates the memory of Monique Lewis, girlfriend to Izzy Stradlin, with Axl also smitten with her, resulting in typical GN'R drama. "Don't Cry" reached #10 on the Billboard 100 and remains a classic rock radio staple to this day.

"Perfect Crime" is high-octane punk metal, again, made tough by Matt's slamming snare and trashed cymbals. Axl's unholy howl, coupled with his rapid-fire enunciation, adds to the song's frantic, chaotic, and even transgressive nature. "You Ain't the First" widens the range, with Guns going bluegrass like Black Crowes or Lynyrd Skynyrd in ballad mode. "Bad Obsession" is bluesy too, featuring cowbell and saloon piano, as well as harmonica and tenor sax courtesy of Michael Monroe from Hanoi Rocks. It's another dose of sleazy Aerosmith—in other words, exactly what this band does in their sleep, although with this one we're getting an influence from that band's self-titled debut or maybe *Get Your Wings*. "Back Off Bitch" is more of the same, albeit speaking to a striding beyond Aerosmith into something a little more squarely heavy metal. It's a co-write by Axl and his childhood buddy Paul Tobias from the early '80s. At the lyric end, it's another one about an old girlfriend, Gina Siler, who finally had enough of Axl and kicked him to the curb back in 1983.

Also heavy metal, solo Izzy credit "Double Talkin' Jive" delivers one of the band's smartest riffs, propelled by a sort of military snare-based beat from Matt that nonetheless grooves. Again, it's the guitar sound that is like a drill bit to the head, intrusive, unforgiving, and distinctly associated with Slash as opposed to Izzy. Speaking of Izzy, his laconic opening vocal, "Found a head and an arm in a garbage can," refers to the fact that the cops had found body parts in a dumpster close by the studio, rumored to be from porn actor Billy London. A very cool feature of this track is that as the song goes into its long, gradual fade, Slash emerges playing flamenco-styled acoustic guitar for a full minute to close out the song.

There's a huge shift is style at the halfway point, with the nine-minute grandeur of "November Rain," possibly Axl's greatest achievement and a #3 smash hit single to boot, despite its length and the multi-climactic passages presented. Predictably, it was a war for Axl to get the song done, with the rest of the band still dismayed by ballads, despite the iconic status of "Sweet Child o' Mine." As for the composition, the two-songs-in-one expanse

was influenced by Elton John's "Funeral for a Friend/Love Lies Bleeding," and again, the messaging was that this band was going to reexamine and explore classic rock from the '70s, whether it was AM radio pop or other things first heard in childhood, or the first music that put a boot up yer ass, like *Hair of the Dog* or *Rocks*. Further making this connection, Axl performed "November Rain" with Elton John at the 1992 MTV VMAs.

If the symphonic (and somewhat Christmas-carol-like) "November Rain" wasn't ambitious enough, "The Garden" manages similar suggestions of Led Zeppelin greatness, through an almost prog rock or pop-blues acoustic-based verse, into the angular, crunchy chorus, featuring old tour mate Alice Cooper. "Garden of Eden" and "Don't Damn Me" mark a wrecking ball swing back to the band's unique form of acidic punk metal, unique, again, through the playing and elevated riff writing, but also Axl's demonic voice and the angry, possessed, fast-babble things he does with it.

"Bad Apples" situates the guys in typical heavy metal Rolling Stones mode, with new sixth Gun Dizzy Reed providing another dose of saloon piano. Dizzy and Axl share keyboard duties on the album, with Axl sticking to piano, although he's also credited with synthesizer and plays a little acoustic guitar. "Dead Horse," with Axl doing his best Dan McCafferty, is the same kind of slashing-chord rock 'n' roll from guitars slung low. Closing the album, we get "Coma," at 10:14, the band's longest song ever. Weirdly, this one also fit the sleazy Aerosmith *Draw the Line* vibe of much that came before, except, unsurprisingly, it cycles through a pile of unexpected stylistic and emotional shifts. Also in spirit with *Draw the Line*, it's written by Axl and Slash about their respective drug overdoses. By the end of it, we've been beaten black N' blue, even if there's not time to recover, because there's still *Use Your Illusion II* to deal with.

16
RAW POWER

GN'R issues *Use Your Illusion II*

"Don't get me wrong," begins Duff. "I like the *Illusion* stuff. I listen to it. My wife had a cassette of it in her truck a couple of weeks ago and it was on when I got in the truck, and it was like, 'Shotgun Blues, 'Yesterdays'; there's some great songs on there. But at that point, I mean, it's going to change. With the amount of money we started to make, and yes—men everywhere, people were just sycophants, just people kissing our ass. You can start believing your own hype after awhile, and it's kind of a tragic thing to watch. Not just with our band—I'd seen it all over the place and now I recognize what it is and it's not real healthy. Sure, it's good for your confidence—up to a certain point. But after that it's just not real healthy. And that kind of stuff started happening with all of us but much more so with Axl."

"When we got into *Use Your Illusion*," adds Slash, "which were two really, really hard . . . or one, really, really hard [*laughs*] bunch of songs that were really hard to write, that was more of an accomplishment, because the band was so dislocated at the time. But the playing on that record, just from a lead guitar player point of view, is ten times better all over the place. But it's all completely improv, almost everything on there, so it all sounds very fluid. But it's not as direct and to the point as, say, 'Welcome to the Jungle,' you know what I mean [*laughs*]? Those solos were a definite arrangement type of thing. So, I'm a fan of it, just because I thought it was a very fluid record guitar-playing wise."

Again, there's no shaped sense of contrast to *Use Your Illusion II* against *Use Your Illusion I*. The range is similarly admirable, with shocks to the system at both ends, from nasty alley cat punk metal through to a polite, mainstream cover of Bob Dylan's famous boomer generation song. "We're competing with rock legends," Axl pronounced at the time, and the world is better for him adopting that attitude.

The album opens boldly with a nearly eight-minute piece of music, not the norm when it comes to sequencing. As discussed, "Civil War" represents a parting presence for Steven Adler. At the lyric end, it's a protest song but with a specific memory at its core. Duff recalls as a kid going to a march with his mother in support of Martin Luther King Jr., which inspires the line, "Did you wear the black arm band when they shot the man who said, 'Peace could last forever?'" The song starts with the line "What we've got here is failure to communicate," and more, sampled from the movie *Cool Hand Luke*. Then Axl whistles "Johnny Comes Marching Home" over acoustic guitar and immediately we're in a different world than "Paradise City." As the song progresses, there's bluster along with some of Axl's best singing across his many gears. There's also perennial piano-plinking from Dizzy Reed, which tends to detract from the stadium rock grandeur of

Somewhere in America, summer 1991. Slash described the guitar work on *Use Your Illusion* as "all completely improv, almost everything on there, so it all sounds very fluid."

Matt Sorum's propulsive playing was critical to *Use Your Illusion* tracks like "Yesterdays" and "Shotgun Blues."

the thing. At the end, the guys double up on the time and jam, before the energy dissipates into Jimi Hendrix wah-wah squalls.

Next is "14 Years," sung mainly by Izzy, who sounds approximately like Axl, given an added pinched affectation. It's a casual old timey rock 'n' roll song, with barrelhouse piano on top of a subtle shuffle feel. Lyrically, the song is about the friendship between Axl and Izzy going back to Indiana, and it sure ain't warm and fuzzy. There's piano all over "Yesterdays" as well, with the band turning in a high-functioning hair metal power ballad, driven hard by Matt's drums, with chord changes that send it into a gospel-tinged southern rock zone.

"Knockin' on Heaven's Door" adds fuel to the sales fire of *Illusion II*, not that it needed it. But situated four songs in, the album by this point has delivered three lighter-foisting ballads and another somewhat beige and dour swampy thing in "14 Years." The tempo picks up with "Get in the Ring," but those chords are a bit jolly, like pop punk. As for the lyrics, it's a foul-mouthed song railing against rock critics like Andy Secher, Mick Wall, and Bob Guccione Jr., with the magazines they work for—*Hit Parader*, *Circus*, *Kerrang!*, and *Spin*—also called out.

Also kind of punky is "Shotgun Blues," which is set to a trashy four-on-the-floor beat from Matt. The piano sprinkled on top creates distance from the punk premise and percussion but also serves as a connection to the blues suggested in the titling. Axl is swearing up a storm for the second song in a row, but the music isn't matching that intensity—that's three up-tempo songs at this point and none of them are particularly blessed with much of a guitar riff. Slash has been pretty dismissive of the song, saying that's what the band was like when it was written back in the mid-'80s. Yet, it must be said: this culling of the old and writing new songs too is how Led Zeppelin achieved greatness on *Physical Graffiti*, and as history would have it, the *Illusion* albums would be viewed very favorably years later as well. The idea is that the guys achieved scope here—not only by looking left and right stylistically, but also by traveling back in time to confront their younger selves.

"Breakdown" is interesting and fresh for this band, kind of a Bruce Springsteen joint with its Americana melody (underscored by Slash playing banjo), ebullient, involved at seven minutes, regular time and then double time, surprising with its passages start to its funky finish. It was a tricky song for Matt to get right, but then again by this point, trying to keep up with his new pals, he was partying hard, which is least forgiving on a drummer because he's got to keep the time. It's arguably the band's greatest masterpiece that remains a deep track, and it's credited solely to Axl, who even the naysayers must admit at this point is an artist worth of respect. Adding to the Easter egg narrative of the album, during the closing jam, Axl recites a speech made over the air by disc jockey Super Soul from the 1971 film *Vanishing Point*, just as the main character Kowalski drives headlong into a police roadblock.

The next two songs, "Pretty Tied Up" and "Locomotive," represent traditional Guns N' Roses circa *Appetite* and some of *Illusion I*, and really, moving forward, there's only one other one like this, namely "You Could Be Mine." Perhaps that represents a difference: the first *Illusion* album contains arguably six to eight crunchy GN'R hard rockers, making that record closer to the flame and this one more adventurous. In any event, "Pretty Tied Up" is vintage Gunners metal (cowbell included), despite the amusing sitar at the beginning. Izzy's lyrics mix S&M imagery with musings about what it's like to be in the biggest band in the world, complaining that "I just found a million dollars that someone forgot," and then even more perceptibly, "Once you made that money, it costs more."

"Locomotive" was written by Slash at a house he and Izzy had briefly rented in the Hollywood Hills. It's a strange animal, despite its carnal old-Guns feel. With music by Slash and lyrics grudgingly added by Axl, it should add up to about four minutes, given the quantity and quality of its action-packed parts. But the guys get a little repetitive, taking it past six minutes, after which they add on a psychedelic coda of about two minutes, dragging us to 8:42. The ending is entertaining enough, but it's quite different music, a spirited jam of sorts, with much guitar soloing, added percussion, and vocal vamping from Axl. All told, "Locomotive" is another underappreciated Guns classic, although the song threatens to unravel at the difficult, punctuated chorus section, where Axl's vocal phrasing is at odds with the military rhythm of the music, despite how valiantly Matt tries to hold it together with high-hat whacks.

Next comes "So Fine," a ballad written by Duff in tribute to New York Dolls heroin casualty Johnny Thunders, who had died recently on April 23, 1991. But you'd never know it from the lyrics, which are just really good and oblique and universal. Duff also sings the song and would do so on the ensuing tour, giving Axl a break from bellowing. Duff eerily channels the spirit of Thunders in his glam-tinged vocal, but then again, both rock heroes danced with the same devil, with Duff at this point in bad shape with booze and cocaine. On piano is Howard Teman, whom the band had considered hiring as keyboardist before they decided on Dizzy, who was essentially Axl's pick.

"Estranged" is this record's longest song and sort of a sister track to "November Rain," given that the lyrics of both are inspired by Axl's troubled marriage with Erin Everly. The two nine-minute songs are also associated by being part of a conceptual "Del James series" of videos (all directed by Andy Morahan) that includes "Don't Cry" as part of the set. The video, with a budget reported to be $4 million, didn't come out until December 1993 to coincide with the release of the song as the album's fourth and final single. As for the music, "Estranged" demonstrates the band's ability to keep these long songs interesting, despite much of the music being pretty conservative and the absence of a discernible chorus. Basically, it's a mid-paced ballad, despite big booming drums and pervasive distorted guitar chord washes and lots of stadium rock soloing from Slash, who found the song challenging. But volume aside, it's a ballad from the melody side of things and there's lots of very grand piano-like Elton John—and all of it from Axl and not Dizzy, adding to the personal nature of a song also solely credited to Axl.

"You Could Be Mine" was issued as an advance single, and it had everybody going nuts for the arrival of the record, given its punishing hard rock precision. Issued as a single on June 21, 1991, it was also used in *Terminator 2: Judgment Day* after Arnold Schwarzenegger himself invited the band over for dinner to seal the deal. The writing of the track goes back to the first sessions leading up to *Appetite for Destruction*, and so it's no surprise it rocks so hard. Although it only got to #29 on the Billboard charts, everybody knows the song now. Plus, it made famous the line, "With your bitch slap rappin' and your cocaine tongue, you get nothing done."

Next comes the alternate version of "Don't Cry," which Axl really distinguishes from the more famed version from *Use Your Illusion I* by offering a different, almost jarring vocal melody in the verses and some of the chorus parts as well. Then, if "Locomotive" has a coda, so does *Use Your Illusion II* as a totality, given the weirdness of closing selection "My World." At 1:26, it's more of a joke track, abrasively industrial, almost hardcore hip-hop. Axl says it was recorded on mushrooms, and he's the only Guns N' Roses member on it.

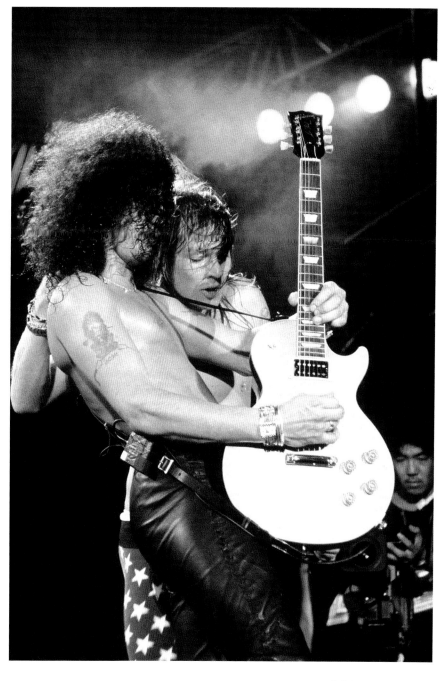

Axl and Slash perform on the first of two nights at the Maracana Stadium, Rock in Rio II festival, Rio de Janeiro, January 15, 1991.

The band gets intimate in Mexico City's 26,000-seat Sports Palace on April 2, 1992.

17
ONE IN A MILLION
Use Your Illusion II debuts at #1

Duff (leaning), Axl (leaning more), and Slash (completely leaned) bring the rock to the masses in spring 1991, a few short months before the release of the *Use Your Illusion* records.

Starting at midnight on September 16 and into the wee hours of September 17, the sensation sloshing around Guns N' Roses' two new albums was, according to Geffen's Eddie Rosenblatt, "the most exciting thing that's ever happened in the record business." He wasn't wrong. Here's a band putting out two new albums after a long wait of four, long, desperate, death-warmed years since their debut, which was now eight-times-platinum—and that was two years ago. Four million copies of the album were shipped and sitting in stores waiting to be sold, with $5 million worth changing hands in the first two hours and between 1.5 and two million units gone in the first week.

Proper history was made when *Use Your Illusion II* entered the Billboard charts at #1 and *Use Your Illusion I* entered the charts at #2, marking the first simultaneous #1 and #2 for any band, and the first time a major artist ever stuck out two new studio albums in one day. Australia, New Zealand, and the UK got in the ring and matched those numbers.

Despite Kmart and Walmart censoring the album off their store shelves—Singapore and South Africa didn't want them either—first-week sales of *II* were pegged at 770,000, with *I* following at 685,000 copies. The second one is thought to have sold better because "You Could Be Mine" from that record was issued as an advance single, and it's a heckuva GN'R song to boot, arguably the rowdiest and most cocksure across all thirty *Illusion* selections.

Doing the grunt work to keep the party going was the single and video release of "Don't Cry," which entered the charts at #76 and then started to climb quickly, reaching #10. Fueling sales in the UK was the band's tribute to Paul McCartney, "Live and Let Die," which reached #5 there, and then into 1992, it hit #33 in the US. Also helping sales is the immense and controversy-filled tour for the albums, but then, maintaining mania, here comes "November Rain" as a single, which, on August 3, 1992, reaches #3 on the charts. Arguably, it's the success of "November Rain" as a radio song and cinematic video that revives the showing of the two records on the charts, reversing a sharp drop by the end of '91 to where *II* ends '92 at #20 and *I*, which contains "November Rain," ends the year at #17.

The RIAA certifications for the *Illusion* duo came fast and furious, and always paired within a few days or weeks of each other. Gold, platinum, and double platinum were all declared on November 19, 1991, with four-times-platinum arriving a year later. The last check for certification was done in 1997, when both records were certified at seven-times-platinum.

Slash brings his top hat—
and Les Paul Gold Top—to
the 1992 MTV Video Music
Awards in Los Angeles.

8
COMA
Izzy's out, Gilby's in

Having gotten sober, Izzy, pictured here in 1990, was less willing to tolerate the crazy GN'R world, especially Axl's controlling nature and tendency to begin shows late.

On August 31, 1991, Guns N' Roses wrapped up a European tour leg in support of their forthcoming two albums, rocking Wembley Stadium in London. Three months of live inactivity would ensue as the band and their fans wrapped their heads around the *Use Your Illusion* records. Come November 27, Axl would make it official, during a Rockline interview, that Izzy Stradlin was out of the band (elsewhere, Slash pegged Izzy's resignation date as November 7). Having cleaned up, Izzy was willing to tolerate less of this crazy world, one major annoyance being Axl's controlling nature and propensity to go on late, sometimes resulting in violence and always resulting in ill will. In addition, Izzy had been presented a contract that diminished his status in the band and chipped into his royalties unless he started contributing more. As Slash framed it, having kicked drugs, Izzy suddenly showed no interest in the band, not doing the videos, not writing, not keeping his chops up, putting more effort into mountain biking. Just three weeks before the next stack of dates, Izzy bailed, sending a letter of resignation to management.

The guys had taken a look at Marc Ford, freshly into the Black Crowes, and Dave Navarro from Jane's Addiction, but Izzy's replacement would be Gilby Clarke, who showed up for the first show after the albums were out, opening a long North American leg in Worcester, Massachusetts, supported by Soundgarden. But you might not have been able to pick out Gilby amid all the traffic onstage: with Dizzy there too, the six-member lineup was now augmented with four backup singers and a three-piece horn section.

Gilby was a natural pick to get in the ring. As he explained to me back in 1999, "When Izzy first came to LA, I was one of the first guys who met him, because there was at first a very small clique of people who grew up on bands like Kiss and Led Zeppelin. But later we got into bands like David Bowie, New York Dolls, and more of the punk stuff like the Clash and Sex Pistols, so there was a small crowd of people who were into rock but then got into the punk rock stuff. And that's how me and Izzy clicked. So him and I were much more compatible with our music. Slash was more about metal."

Gilby had made records with Candy and Kill for Thrills. "Yes, and we were a pop band, but we played with punk rock attitude—it was like early

Beatles [*laughs*]. With Kill for Thrills, I actually started singing as well as playing guitar. But I had known the Guns guys since the Candy days. We had gotten ourselves a major label deal and they were a local band. So when it came time for Izzy to be leaving the band, I got the call from Slash, who said, 'You know, we're looking for a guitar player,' and I obviously said yes and I played with them and I got the gig. They know what they want and I pretty much gelled with the band. We had been playing the same kind of music, same kind of look, same interests, so it was easy for me to step into that. To tell you the truth, I think I was the only guy they auditioned."

Gilby's knowledge of both metal and punk made him a natural choice to replace Izzy.

9
HUMAN BEING
The Freddie Mercury Tribute Concert

Just five months after the death of Britain's most beloved rock star Freddie Mercury, an event was staged that just might be the greatest concert extravaganza of all time. Richer in magic moments than Live Aid, the US Festival, any Rock in Rio, good Woodstocks and bad Woodstocks, or even Queen themselves at Wembley, the *Freddie Mercury Tribute Concert for AIDS Awareness* provided a flood of emotional performances across an innovative framing, consisting of short band sets for the first half and for the second half, Brian May, John Deacon, and Roger Taylor playing Queen classics with big guest stars, a few of who already had appeared during the first opening salvo.

Kicking off the April 20, 1992, Wembley festivities, Metallica crunched through three selections from their blowing-up self-tilted album, issued a month prior to the *Use Your Illusion* barnstormed bookends. Next came Extreme with a Queen medley and their quiet hit, "More than Words." Def Leppard did two of their own, plus "Now I'm Here." Bob Geldof, Spinal Tap, and U2 (via satellite) followed, all with one song each, with the last performance of the first set coming from Guns N' Roses, essentially making them the headliners of a four-band package, all from the hard rock world.

The Gunners showed up in deluxe mode, augmented by their three backup singers (with Teddy Andreadis also serving as second keyboardist), and Slash tipping his hat to the Brits with a Rolling Stones shirt and Axl seconding that motion, wearing a custom Union Jack jacket. First came a tight "Paradise City," locked down by Matt's exacting drum work but let loose by Axl and Slash, who were both on fire, darting about the stage. For the second and last selection, we got the unpredictable rock 'n' roll moment, where not only did the band stretch time and deliver a 9:00 version of "Knockin' on Heaven's Door," but they opened with a verse of Alice Cooper's "Only Women Bleed," with Axl singing seated.

The Guns N' Roses performance is widely considered the apex of the first set, but, incredibly, it would be Axl all on his own that provided some of the most cherished moments of the concluding Queen set, galvanized in rock 'n' roll history along with Annie

Lennox's and David Bowie's performance of "Under Pressure" and then George Michael's thrilling collaboration with the guys on "Somebody to Love." Axl appears twice, on "We Will Rock You" and "Bohemian Rhapsody," and it is on the latter that he so resplendently mattered.

But there lingered the nagging narrative of the "One in a Million" controversy, where Axl railed against homosexuals, lumping them in with criminals. Now the band, curiously and provocatively, was one of only four acts chosen to open a show for AIDS awareness. Justifying matters, Axl was a massive Freddie Mercury and Queen fan and also a huge Elton John fan, and here he appeared singing a duet with the Rocket Man on Queen's most famous song.

Still, there was an undercurrent of rock 'n' roll tension, typical GN'R menace, infecting the event. When Elton knocked on Axl's dressing room to summon him to rehearsal, a security guard answered and said, "Axl's sleeping" and shut the door in Elton's face. There would be no rehearsal, and everybody was walking on eggshells, wondering if the meeting of the generations would even take place.

But Axl—again, all on his own, with no other Gunners required—did indeed turn up and was there for three iconic filmed rock 'n' roll flashes across all time. The first is his arrival onstage to the headbanging bit of "Bohemian Rhapsody." In he bounds, twirling, kilted and kitted to the Axl nines, chopped mic stand, after which he sings his part dead-accurate, passionate, reverent, but expectedly so, because he is always respectful of other bands' material. It's still talked about as one of the greatest entrances of all time. Adding to the mania, he confidently leaps onto a monitor howling, and then down again, not missing a beat.

Second, as that section ends, he tosses down his mic stand, and mesmerized, he walks toward Brian. Out comes Elton John, understated in a red jacket and quiet hair and glasses, and the two walk in unison up to the lip of the stage. At that first "Nothing really matters"—oddly, Metallica played "Nothing Else Matters" way back at the beginning of the evening—Roger Taylor breaks out into a gushing laugh and smile of ebullient emotion. He watches on intently and then can't help but smile again as Elton and Axl look at each other with total reverence and respect during the shared, "Nothing really matters to me."

There's a third magic moment to come, as Axl stares, lost in thought, close into the crowd before his final vocal. He then turns, on cue, to Elton for the final "Any way the wind blows" and then we are done, any ill will now washed water under the bridge.

The Easter Monday event in front of seventy-two thousand loud and very happy attendees was broadcast live to another billion or so fans worldwide in an estimated seventy-six countries. Sadly, it represented the reclusive John Deacon's last full show with Brian and Roger. But on the brighter side, proceeds from the event helped establish the Mercury Phoenix Trust, an AIDS charity that exists to this day, with both Brian and Roger as trustees.

Elton and Axl at the
Freddie Mercury Tribute,
April 20, 1992. A
performance for the ages.

Slash jams with Brian May at the *Freddie Mercury Tribute Concert*—two guitarists with their own distinct sounds and styles.

A few dozen of the world's top rockers—plus Liza Minnelli— take a bow at the finale of the *Freddie Mercury Tribute Concert* at London's Wembley Stadium.

8/25

20
CIVIL WAR
Chaos at Metallica/Guns N' Roses show in Montreal

Eight shows into a sold-out stadium tour with Metallica and assorted backups, Axl was already experiencing vocal issues, had thrown up onstage (and started the song again), and had been hit in the crotch with a lighter during "Knockin' on Heaven's Door." Slash had even cautioned the *Montreal Gazette* that Axl had a "hole in his vocal cord," but that the "typhoon of chaos" surrounding the band wouldn't stop the show. But the band's visit to Montreal's beleaguered Olympic Stadium spelled double doom. With Faith No More having played a full forty-five-minute set and Metallica rounding the corner on their set—eighty minutes and ten songs in and just starting "Fade to Black"—James Hetfield found himself briefly engulfed in flames during an errant pyro incident, causing burns to his leg, arm, hand, and face. As he was rushed to the hospital, Lars approached the mic and promised a makeup show, which in fact turned into two half-price shows in February the following year.

What ensued was a two-and-a-half-hour wait for the Guns to take the stage, after which there were concerns from the band with respect to hearing themselves properly out of the monitors, which Slash said were feeding back the whole time. The band made it through "It's So Easy," "Mr. Brownstone," "Live and Let Die," "Attitude," "Nightrain," "Perfect Crime," and "Bad Obsession" before Axl told the crowd, "We got it together in Europe only to have it come apart here. In case anyone is interested, this is gonna be our last show for a long time." But Axl's main complaint seemed to be his voice, and as he explained afterward, he took Slash aside and told him he'd keep trying, but if it didn't work, he was going to have to quit; otherwise, he'd likely be damaging his throat permanently. They muddled through "Double Talkin' Jive" and "Civil War," but with Axl's continued vocal pain and a quick agreement that nobody could hear themselves, they decided to throw in the towel after having played for about fifty-five minutes. I mentioned that the building was "beleaguered." Indeed, Slash even seemed to blame Canada's so-called The Big Owe, remarking, "Nothing against the people of Montreal; we had a great time hanging out there. I think it was the building itself."

As the house lights went on, about 2,000 of the 52,666 in attendance that night began to riot, smashing windows, setting fires, and looting the merch area. The melee continued outdoors where the crowd uprooted a streetlight and overturned a police car. Once the smoke—and tear gas—cleared, three officers had been injured and about a dozen arrests had been made. But despite the limited personal injury, estimated damages reached up to $1 million.

The tour continued August 25 through October 6, after a half dozen postponements and a cancelation in Vancouver, with James relegated to vocal duties and John Marshall from Metal Church picking up James's guitar parts. According to Slash, Metallica and Guns N' Roses would get the same paycheck, but his band would barely break even due to Axl incurring heavy fines for going on late and then throwing lavish, themed parties afterward, ostensibly to show the guys in Metallica who's boss.

Metallica's James Hetfield tends to the scars suffered when he strayed into the path of pyrotechnics during the Montreal concert with Guns N' Roses.

1999
GN'R issues *Live Era '87–'93*
November 23

2004
Geffen issues *Greatest Hits*
March 23

2006
Izzy Stradlin rejoins the band
(sort of)
May 17

2008
Dr Pepper announces a campaign
linked to the release of *Chinese
Democracy*
March 26

2012
Guns N' Roses are inducted into the
Rock & Roll Hall of Fame
April 14

2016
Guns N' Roses mounts their
first reunion-era tour
April 8

2022
Geffen issues expanded
editions of the *Use Your
Illusion* albums
November 11

2023
New single "Perhaps"/"The General"
generates hope for a
new GN'R album soon
December 8

1983
Hollywood Rose forms

June

1985
Guns N' Roses plays their first ever show, at the Troubadour in Hollywood, California

March 26

1985
Slash and Steven Adler join Guns N' Roses, completing the classic lineup

June 4

1986
GN'R signs with Geffen Records

March 25

1988
Guns N' Roses performs at Monsters of Rock, Castle Donington

August 20

1988
GN'R issues *GN'R Lies*

November 29

1989
The first of four shows supporting the Rolling Stones

October 18

1990
Farm Aid IV, drummer Steven Adler's last show with the band

April 7

1991
GN'R issues *Use Your Illusion I*

September 17

1991
GN'R issues *Use Your Illusion II*

September 17

1991
Use Your Illusion II debuts at #1 on the US charts, followed by *Use Your Illusion I*

October 5

1991
It is announced that Izzy Stradlin has left the band

November 7

1986
GN'R issues
Live ?!@ Like a Suicide*
December 16

1987
GN'R issues *Appetite for Destruction*
July 21

1987
GN'R embarks upon their first North American tour
August 14

1988
Appetite for Destruction hits #1 in the US
August 6

1990
Soundtrack cover "Knockin' on Heaven's Door" features the GN'R debut of Matt Sorum
June 26

1991
A miffed Axl Rose leaves the stage midshow in St. Louis, causing a riot
July 2

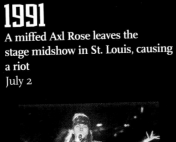

1992
The band performs at *The Freddie Mercury Tribute Concert for AIDS Awareness*
April 20

1992
Chaos ensues at a joint Metallica/Guns N' Roses show in Montreal
August 8

1993
Appetite for Destruction is certified ten-times-platinum in the US
March 25

1993
GN'R issues *"The Spaghetti Incident?"*
November 23

1996
Axl announces that Slash is no longer a part of GN'R
October 30

1999
A new GN'R song, "Oh My God," appears on the *End of Days* soundtrack
November 2

2008
Steven Adler records his first episode of *Celebrity Rehab with Dr. Drew*
October 23

2008
GN'R issues *Chinese Democracy*
November 23

2009
GN'R embarks on their first tour after the release of *Chinese Democracy*
December 11

2012
The band embarks on the Up Close and Personal tour
February 10

2016
Axl is in AC/DC!
May 7

2018
Appetite for Destruction is the subject of an elaborate reissue program
June 29

2021
The band embarks on the We're F'N' Back! tour
July 31

2021
GN'R issues "Absurd," followed by "Hard Skool"
August 6

Axl works the crowd at Foxborough, Massachusetts, September 11, 1992.

21
I.R.S.
Appetite for Destruction certified ten-times-platinum in the US

Guns N' Roses had just played Winnipeg, Manitoba, and were en route to Saskatoon, Saskatchewan, when, on March 25, 1993, they got the news that the RIAA had just certified *GN'R Lies* at four-times-platinum and *Appetite for Destruction* at an astounding ten-times-platinum. The band played Edmonton next and then Vancouver, closing out a Canadian leg of the grinding *Use Your Illusion* tour before dipping back into the US on April 1.

However, the band's career-defining debut didn't officially become a diamond album until that designation was codified by a party held on March 16, 1999, at the Roseland Ballroom in New York City. Forty-six artists were celebrated on that day, among them, recent tourmates Metallica, who had surpassed ten million in 1997. Hometown heroes Van Halen also were feted at the party, and for two albums, *Van Halen* and *1984*, although it's interesting to note that *Appetite for Destruction* beat both those records to ten million, with the debut getting there in 1996 and *1984* in 1999.

In fact, while Elton John, Kenny Rogers, Kenny G, Billy Joel, and MC Hammer, along with members of AC/DC, Boston, Def Leppard, Journey, Boys II Men, Led Zeppelin, and ZZ Top, were living it up at the Roseland, only one member of Guns N' Roses was on hand to accept the award. That was Steven Adler, recently off a 150-day stint in LA County Jail for assaulting a girlfriend. By that point, Guns N' Roses was no more, with Axl, on February 18, pleading guilty to a misdemeanor charge of

disturbing the peace, generated by an incident at the Phoenix airport. Also, Duff and Matt were gearing up for three performances, beginning April 5, as part of the Neurotic Outsiders, which also featured Steve Jones from the Sex Pistols and John Taylor from Duran Duran—Duff also had a new band called Loaded. But just a couple months earlier, Duff, Matt, and Slash performed together at a film festival, eliciting hope of a GN'R reunion.

On a brighter note, as Steven accepted the Diamond Award in New York, *Appetite for Destruction* had in fact just surpassed fifteen million in sales. And although there hasn't been an official certification past eighteen-times-platinum, achieved in 2008, chances are that with streaming numbers for the album's three biggest hits past one billion each on Spotify alone, a new accounting likely would find *Appetite for Destruction* past double-diamond. Additionally, the album is already past twenty-two million sold based on global certifications, with estimated sales over and above the achieved award levels—bringing it to an estimated thirty million copies worldwide.

As for March 25, 1993, it was just another day on the road for Guns N' Roses, situated at the beginning of a leg of *Illusion* they'd called the Skin N' Bones tour. After playing much of April in America and Mexico, there was a long stint in Europe, punctuated by two mid-July dates in Argentia, after which it all blew up.

Slash channels Eddie Van Halen at the National Bowl, Milton Keynes, Buckinghamshire, England, on May 30, 1993, a week after getting the news *Appetite for Destruction* had achieved 10-times-platinum status.

Opposite: While GN'R was one of the acts being feted by the industry for achieving diamond status with *Appetite for Destruction*, Matt (barely visible at far left) and Duff were gearing up for shows with their Neurotic Outsiders side project featuring John Taylor of Duran Duran (second from right) and Steve Jones of the Sex Pistols (far right).

2

ATTITUDE

GN'R releases "The Spaghetti Incident?"

Appetite for Destruction caught fire because it felt real, because these guys drank deeply of both the trash city rock 'n' roll lifestyle and rock 'n' roll itself. The mark of a rock 'n' roll lover is how much they want to play DJ, and the Gunners were always like that. Like many Hollyrockers, their initial foothold in the accursed business was through covers, and then once making records, they carried on proselytizing about music they loved, telling people about Rose Tattoo and suggesting a lineage back to Aerosmith, whose obscure debut-era track "Mama Kin" became a highlight of the band's first EP. Time grinds on and they contributed significantly to rock history with their own songs, but you could still count on the band to pull out an obscure cover live. Plus, "Knockin' on Heaven's Door" was soon to become one of their biggest hits, and the band's take on "Sympathy for the Devil" made a dent as well.

Issued November 23, 1993, *"The Spaghetti Incident?"* began life fully authentically, like so much of the music painfully birthed by these troubled souls. The guys would do covers just to sober up across the expanse of the *Use Your Illusion* sessions. Soon the idea formulated that they might issue a handful of them as an EP, just like the old days. In tandem with the project growing into a full album, there was the band's ongoing enthusiasm to tell their fans about obscure music they loved, but also the idea that it might make some these suffering artists a few bucks in royalties.

In that light, the guys batted around *Pension Fund* as a working title, but they went with *"The Spaghetti Incident?"* because of an amusing exchange that took place when Steven Adler had been suing GN'R for more cash. It seems that when the band were holed up in Chicago for a spell, Steven kept his drug stash in a takeout container in the fridge next to the real leftover takeout, with his contraband jokingly referred to as spaghetti. Later in court, Steven's legal council asked the band to tell them about the spaghetti incident, which they found amusing. This is how we end up with the quote marks and the question mark in the title, which probably lopped 15 percent off the potential sales of the album, because it was too much of a pain to write about and even say. Are you supposed to raise your voice at the end? And now that you have, do you have to have a debate about why you said it that way? Then there's the stomach-churning album cover, basically wall-to-wall spaghetti that looks like it's out of a can.

The album opens with "Since I Don't Have You," a Skyliners cover, which fools us into thinking we might be in for something akin to the *Honeydrippers* EP from Robert and Jimmy nine years earlier. But then we're into a blazing version of "New Rose" from the Damned, presented with carnal arch-Slash guitar tones and swinging, stadium rock drumming from Matt, representing

the biggest difference on the song, given the manic Keith Moon chaos that Rat Scabies provides on the 1977 original. Next is the UK Subs' "Down on the Farm," which builds on "New Rose" by moving us forward in punk history through the song's UK hardcore chord changes—famously, Guns had presented this one live at Farm Aid. Matt is also there to straighten out two proto-punk songs, "Human Being" from the New York Dolls circa '74 and "Raw Power" from Igg and the Stooges circa '73. The first punk leg ends with a cover of "Ain't It Fun" from the second and last Dead Boys album. It's a perfect pick for the Gunners, due to its grim and biting lyrics and it's spooky, despondent, soft-then-heavy ballad structure, perfected on the *Use Your Illusion* albums. Plus, it's just a cool and obscure pick. Band buddy Michael Monroe provides co-lead vocals.

The rest of the album is a messy grab bag. First, there's T.Rex/Soundgarden tape-job "Buick Makane (Big Dumb Sex)," followed by a sincere rendition of Nazareth anthem "Hair of the Dog." Next is a minute-and-a-half Misfits song, a melodic churn, neither here nor there, followed by a track by Steve Jones (and not the Sex Pistols) and Johnny Thunders (and not the New York Dolls). Both are gems and for entirely different reasons. As Slash has correctly pointed out, "Black Leather" is performed with more lust gusto here than it was originally, and it really becomes a typical, raucous GN'R joint. "You Can't Put Your Arms Around a Memory" is just a lovable song no matter who does it, but it's particularly poignant here, given its druggy origins and its wistful sentiment. Plus, as

a sort of Phil Spector pageant, it fits Axl's ambitions. The album ends with "I Don't Care About You," a short Fear cover, which essentially completes a three-part hardcore subnarrative along with the UK Subs and Misfits songs.

There's a hidden thirteenth track, and that's a haunting cover of a Charles Manson song called "Look at Your Game, Girl." With the label defending it as the product of the band's dark humor, the choice predictably caused consternation. Making things right, Geffen donated the royalties associated with the track to the Doris Tate Crime Victims Bureau, set up in tribute to the slain Sharon Tate.

"The Spaghetti Incident?" would be the only Guns N' Roses album to feature Gilby Clarke as part of the lineup, although some of Izzy Stradlin's guitar parts had been retained as well. The album was not toured, which might have something to do with it stalling at platinum, albeit within two months of release. Furthermore, "Ain't It Fun," issued as a single, was not fun, and "Since I Don't Have You," also pushed, was more of a joke, an "ironic" cover.

The band receives their Michael Jackson Video Vanguard Award for "November Rain" at the MTV Video Music Awards on September 10, 1992. Presenters Brian May and Roger Taylor of Queen are barely visible in the background. At the podium from left: Duff McKagan, Gilby Clarke, Axl, Slash, Dizzy Reed, and Matt Sorum.

Axl performs at Milton Keynes in a shirt bearing the image of Charles Manson. Six months later, the band's covers album would include one of the cult leader's songs as a hidden track.

Axl and Michael Monroe perform at the Whisky a Go Go in Hollywood on December 12, 1989. Monroe has been framed as a sort of Axl Rose prototype for his work with the Finnish glam band Hanoi Rocks.

23

YOU AIN'T THE FIRST

Axl announces that Slash has left

Side projects, guest appearances, arrests, and near-death experiences seemed to be the domain of various Guns N' Roses members through the mid-'90s. But then the suspected discombobulation of the band became real when, on October 30, 1996, Axl fired off a fax to MTV with numbered points falling into roughly three categories. Items #1 through #5 kicked off the screed with Axl essentially explaining that Guns N' Roses will now become an underground band. Item #6 turned the tables, though, promising a new record. Then came Item #7, which stated that Slash "will not be involved in any Guns N' Roses endeavors."

Credit to both parties, really, that a complicated and almost chess-like case of musical differences blew the thing up, although an equally complex clash of personal pathologies was always there, poisoning the well.

As far as Slash was concerned, the guitarist had proven he was in it for the right reasons, jamming with anybody that would have him, including Paul Rodgers, Peter Green, and Zakk Wylde's band, Pride and Glory—note that Zakk was briefly considered as a protentional GN'R hire. He had played James Brown's sixty-third birthday party and appeared onstage with Michael Jackson at the MTV Music Video Awards. Most significantly, he had formed a band called Slash's Snakepit and made a record, with both Gilby and Matt and producer Mike Clink from the Gunners, called *It's Five O'Clock Somewhere*. The album essentially exists because Slash was writing for the next GN'R album, and the end result sounds like a GN'R record, the significant difference being the inclusion of Eric Dover from Jellyfish as frontman and cowriter on most of the songs.

But going back to the summer of 1994, Axl wasn't buying into Slash's new material. Or he was and he wasn't. As he frames it, he wanted to work with these songs and with Slash, but he was also going to be significantly discerning, discarding parts and whole songs, trying to evolve them and to continue to take GN'R on a path past *Appetite* into the pantheon of the greats, like the Stones, Queen, and Led Zeppelin. Matt Sorum has said as much, implying that *It's Five O'Clock Somewhere* exists because Axl didn't think the songs were good enough. As far as Slash is concerned, he wanted more of a tough, basic rock 'n' roll album and explained that Axl wanted to take the band industrial, citing Axl's admiration for Nine Inch Nails. But ask Axl, and he would frame it as a will to use only the best of the best, and sure, to experiment, to take the songs further.

But egos also were involved with control of the band beyond the music being an issue. As well-meaning battles over songwriting continued, Axl was miffed that Slash was overexposing himself, undermining the unity of the band, with what he perceived as a flashy public presence. Simultaneously, Axl was unilaterally replacing band members, with Slash at one point trying to make it work by signing on in a reduced role, only to change his mind twenty-four hours later. The new personnel, and Axl's radical opinions on the music, pointed in the same direction as far as Slash was concerned—that Axl was losing the plot, or maybe losing his mind.

In Axl's defense, his public statements seemed rational, measured, even diplomatic. He complimented Slash, implying that only he could write the riffs worthy of making the next Guns N' Roses album, as he put it, the Aerosmith *Rocks* of 1996. Framing it that way demonstrates that the two were somewhat on the same page, especially given that when they were young and hungry, they had collaborated on the *Rocks* of 1987. But in the next breath, Axl would imply that great riffs don't guarantee

The ex-GN'R guitar slinger performs in Milan, Italy, in December 2000 as the namesake of Slash's Snakepit.

Slash and Eric Dover, at a pre-press conference photo session in Milan, Italy

great songs, and now the real work begins. Also, to Axl's credit, his instincts proved correct, with Slash's Snakepit, in the end, putting something together that was closer to *Done with Mirrors* than *Rocks*, namely tough, bluesy, purist rock 'n' roll that was, to be sure, valiantly *Appetite*-like but ultimately unsatisfying, not surprising enough.

What ensued was a long and complicated legal divorce, with Axl buying the rights to the Guns N' Roses name in January 1997 and Slash touring under the moniker Slash's Blues Ball. Meanwhile, Duff also was exiled and on his own trip, with an unsurprising solo album of his own as well as a record with the Neurotic Outsiders (featuring Slash's Snakepit drummer Matt Sorum!). McKagan almost died when his pancreas exploded on May 10, 1994. Band buddy Shannon Hoon was less lucky, passing away from an overdose on Halloween in 1995, with another friend of the band, songwriter West Arkeen, also overdosing on May 30, 1997.

Typical of the band's sense of mystery, misfire, and miscommunication, there would be no further clarification on the Slash situation until November 1999, when Axl opened up to MTV on the issue, saying that it had been a three-and-a-half-year process of trying to work things out with Slash. True to the spirit of what caused the divide in the first place, even when the two eventually did patch things up, there would be ample touring and hugs all around, but no new album.

Slash performs with Michael Jackson at the MTV Video Awards in New York City, September 7, 1995.

24
GARDEN OF EDEN

New GN'R song appears on *End of Days* soundtrack

Rock in Rio, Rio de Janeiro, January 14, 2001

As the first song in five years and first original song in eight years, "Oh My God" counts as a significant sign that Guns N' Roses exists. The occasion was the *End of Days* soundtrack album, which was full of a bunch of cutting-edge modern hard rock, industrial, and hip-hop acts. True to Axl's consistent vision now for a good four years, his new-look Guns N' Roses emphatically fit right in.

Across the paragraphs of an admirably articulate essay he had written to *Rolling Stone* about the song, Axl talks about how his lyrics for it combine a deep tissue massage of his personality and psychology as it relates to his struggles with fame, free will, and free speech, with inspiration from the movie itself "and its metaphors." He also takes no credit for the music, but we get to see how radical he's being about who is in the band now and how confirmed both Slash and Duff are about the direction Axl is taking the brand.

Writing the song, according to the dissertation, are Paul Huge primarily and Dizzy Reed on the chorus. The official writing credit includes those two (aka Paul Tobias and Darren Arthur Reed), along with Josh Freese, Tommy Stinson (from the

Replacements), and Sean Riggs, sometimes Guns drummer and Dizzy's roommate. Playing on the song are Paul, Tommy, Dizzy, and Josh, but also Chris Pitman on keyboards and synths, plus two additional guitarists in Gary Sunshine and Dave Navarro. Gary had done some sessions with Axl at his home and then was called in to play rhythms. He had been in a privileged position to watch Axl's creative life at this juncture, seeing him toil away on new music, quite reclusive, but kind and respectful and seriously wanting to work as an artist. As for Dave Navarro, Axl had always been a huge Jane's Addiction fan since their demo and had now finally been able to work with Dave, although it was basically an hour-and-a-half studio session to peel off a guitar solo. Additional programming and audio manipulation was done by engineer Stuart White, while Axl credits the departed Robin Finck as appearing on the track, although he wants to make it known that Finck was not in on the writing and that his parts were significantly modified by the producer.

In his *Rolling Stone* screed, Axl thanks Arnold Schwarzenegger for the opportunity and also made it clear that Interscope producer Jimmy Iovine was involved, although the main production credit goes to Sean Beavan, who had a long history with Nine Inch Nails. He also lets it be known that Duff and Matt "failed to see the potential" of the song, again confirming the Axl was on a different creative path than the rest of the old Gunners, which is why he was now firing ideas off a new gang of pirates.

The result is something of a minor masterpiece, a thoughtful but heavy song, even a little punky and thrashy, with one of the oddest chimera-like shape shifts between traditional hard rock and industrial I've ever heard attempted and then intriguingly executed. The drumbeat is punishing and tribal, whether it's at the panic-stricken verses or the pounding choruses, which are performed at half-time to the verse. There's also a sort of industrial dance beat section, similarly full up with both heavy metal and electronic sounds, which serves as

disorienting break music. Then there's new music again for the guitar solo. The song is over and done with in under four minutes, but it's a draining experience.

Adding to the complicated history of "Oh My God," in 2008 Axl called it an unfinished demo, rushed to fruition so that it could be delivered on time for the soundtrack album. Axl also said that there's an alternate remixed version, which makes total sense given the spirit of experimentation at the time. Frantic and screechy as it is, it's hard to picture "Oh My God" as a demo, given how many layers of noises can be discerned within it. This characteristic extends to Axl's vocals as well, which are sometimes distorted, adding to the industrial vibe. The song was never issued as a stand-alone single, but it got ample press notices (and mixed reviews), with the album reaching #20 on the Billboard charts and certifying platinum. "Oh My God" was first played live on January 1, 2001, at the House of Blues in Las Vegas, but it's represented for posterity on YouTube through an aggressive performance captured at Rock in Rio two weeks later in front of a crowd of two hundred thousand.

Although beginning its run on radio a month-and-a-half before the release of the movie, and despite it appearing in the trailer, which was played at the MTV Video Music Awards, "Oh My God" never charted, lasting on the airwaves about five weeks. Ultimately, what we got out of the song was an acclimatization as to who Guns N' Roses were now, and, remarkably enough, through the next dozen years. In fact, underscoring multiple testimonies to Axl's sense of loyalty, despite the dizzying number of people it would take to make both "Oh My God" and *Chinese Democracy*, many of the same players would be there for both projects and the touring, irrespective of what must have been trying times getting the eventual full-length album constructed and birthed.

A fan's perspective of Rock in Rio, 2001

25
LIVE AND LET DIE

GN'R issues *Live Era '87–'93*

In typical languished fashion, Guns N' Roses finally made use of the fact that, as Axl put it, they'd recorded every show on the *Use Your Illusion* tour, along with tons of backstage footage, in hopes that they'd make a documentary of the experience. Now that the band had disintegrated, and Axl was "on his own trip," as Slash framed it, it was decided that with the Interscope MCA merger completed and the band owning records on their contract, it might be time to put the brand back into the public eye in any manner possible. More than that, though, the idea was to put the classic long-gone band and all those smash hits back in the spotlight.

And the guys took it seriously, listening to a lot of tapes, picking songs, and working on mixes with Andy Wallace. But communication with Axl was through notes. Duff and Slash would work on mixes during the day and leave comments for Axl, who would come in at night. Slash was overt in his insistence that the album was GN'R warts and all, taking him back to records like *Get Yer Ya-Ya's Out!* from the Stones, *At Budokan* by Cheap Trick, and *Live! Bootleg* from Aerosmith, but Duff blabbed about fixes, with the consensus being that some rerecording of vocals had gotten done.

The packaging sure wasn't telling. In fact, the front cover was slathered in ancient gig flyers, suggesting that this was going to be significantly archival. Then there was the messy title—if anything, these were songs from the band's recording "era." I mean, if you are going to say something weird like "live era," well, I suppose this is a band you can talk about in those terms, but then you'd be putting out songs from after 2012, wouldn't you? Again, if anything, these are live songs from the band's cherished and short-lived recording era! Moving on from that minor irritation, open the booklet and we're told only that these songs were "recorded across the universe between 1987 and 1993." Technically that's true—there's one from '87, two from '88, three from '91, fifteen from '92, and one from '93—but the implication is that there'd be more Steven Adler.

Which brings up a new issue, namely that the band is presented in the booklet as Axl, Slash, Duff, Dizzy, Izzy, and Steven. Matt Sorum and Gilby Clarke, who play on almost all of it, are partitioned out as "additional musicians." To be sure, the real additional musicians are listed as well, but therein lies another problem—the brunt of this album reminds us that the guys were traveling with a second keyboardist, a horn section, and backing female vocals, muddying the attack of some of these songs, which already suffer from what they call brickwalling, or the loudness wars, a sort of "everything up in the mix" trend at the time that tends to cause listener fatigue.

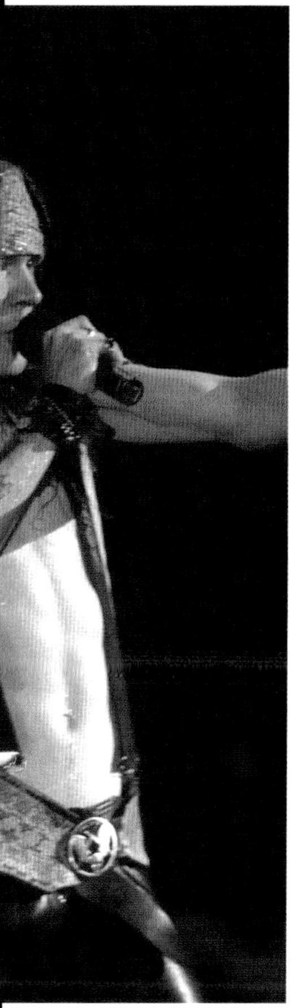

The classic period got a revisit in 1999 with the release of *Live Era '87–'93.*

As for the track list, folks complained about the absence of "Civil War," but other than that, it's a pretty laudable set. Across twenty-two tracks and two CDs, we get challenging, ambitious things like "November Rain" and "Estranged," along with the two most slammin' tracks from the *Illusion* records, namely "Pretty Tied Up" and "You Could Be Mine." *Illusion* also yields the magnificent "Don't Cry" and "Yesterdays" on the ballad end, while we also get "Knockin' on Heaven's Door," chuckled at by fans and the press for the reggae jam, but welcome nonetheless and not too crazy-long at 7:27. Good to see "Patience" and "Move to the City" included for historical value and all of *Appetite* is there, save for "Think About You" and "Anything Goes."

Most surprising and certainly welcome is a solo performance by Axl, singing and playing piano, on a poignant version of "It's Alright," drummer Bill Ward's song on Black Sabbath's *Technical Ecstasy*. Also surprising is the choosing of "Coma" for the Japanese bonus track, given how complicated it is and how few times the band ever played it. In fact, Slash has divulged that he and Izzy had to write up elaborate cheat sheets to use onstage to figure out what keys and chords to play at the end of the thing.

There wasn't much hoopla surrounding *Live Era '87–'93*, with the first word of it emerging May 15, 1999, six months before its November 23 release date. Once out, there were basically no interviews done for it and little promotion from the label, which irked Slash. For his part, Axl stuck the nail in the coffin expressing that it was a goodbye to the old band, who, he claims, he could hear dying on the album, which made revisiting these songs painful for the last Gunner standing. As a result, the album reached only gold in terms of certification (and this despite counting its two discs as two units) and was soon off the charts, after entering at #45. Two weeks after the album showed up in stores, Big F D Entertainment, the band's management company, sued Slash and Duff, claiming monies were owed.

"The cool thing about it is that it sounds good and it's real," Slash said back in 2000. "It came out of the box and all the fans got it, so it's cool. It would have been great if Guns, at that particular point, was together and touring. The album would have been amazingly huge. But there was no reality in that. So how to work a Guns N' Roses record when the band's not together and Axl's on some trip? I can't give you an answer—make it up; use your imagination."

Duff, Steven, and Axl, at the Ritz in New York City, October 23, 1987 (main); early-days Duff and Izzy in So-Cal (inset).

Hair of the Dog

GN'R VERSUS HAIR METAL

I wade into this section of our story as an admitted skeptic, of the opinion from day one that Guns N' Roses was most definitely part of the hair metal movement, albeit representing a shift for the better. That's my assertion, that they changed it from within, rather than what Soundgarden or Nirvana did, which was change it from without. An important adjunct to that is that the Seattle scene caused the death of hair metal, whereas GN'R actually caused a second wind, three more years of Hollyrock, spawning bands of similar fashion, gritty heaviness and swampy bluesiness. Then again, the Gunners' knowledge of and love for classic '70s hard rock, along with the injection of punk attitude, could be viewed as a springboard or gateway drug to grunge, which more overtly professed to meld those influences. But enough of what I think. Following are a few quotes on the subject from those who were more "boots on the ground" than I was.

Nuno Bettencourt, Extreme

"I have to be careful with that term 'hair metal' [*laughs*]. You know what? I think the first band we really noticed that was doing less of what maybe Poison and Warrant were doing was Guns N' Roses. I think Guns N' Roses were going back to the Aerosmith side of things, that version of it, which was definitely more punk and rock combined. I think that was the first hint."

Extreme, left to right:
Gary Cherone, Nuno
Bettencourt, Pat
Badger, and Paul
Geary (crouched), Los
Angeles, February 1989

Billy Childs, Britny Fox

"Guns N' Roses, when they first came out, they were very much a hair band. People seem to forget that. But they immediately saw what was going on, and I mean, they got dirty real quick. It's funny—it wasn't just us that got caught up in all this. I don't think grunge killed hair metal. Hair metal committed suicide. There were too many bad bands, too many guys who couldn't play, too many guys who couldn't sing, and it just got really bad."

Billy Childs performs with his band Britny Fox at the Orpheum Theatre in Minneapolis, March 23, 1990.

Kevin Estrada, photographer

"Guns N' Roses came out of that whole kitchen of hair metal. We had Hollywood Rose and we had the L.A. Guns guys. When Guns N' Roses started, they were wearing makeup and they were wearing fishnets and they were very glammy, but musically they weren't doing what those glam bands were doing. They weren't writing mostly love ballads. Those other bands were putting out ten ballads and two rock songs. Guns N' Roses was doing ten rock songs and two ballads, and even their ballads weren't cheesy ballads aimed at girls. The music they were writing was universal. Guys and girls connected with this band. Guns N' Roses were real. It wasn't about, 'Hey, I look great; I'm going to start a band.' They were in the band because they loved music, they were great musicians, and music was in their blood. They just happened to start while that scene was blooming and that's what was around, and they came out looking like the environment that they were in. But musically they were far superior and in a whole different galaxy than these glam bands, and that's what separated them.

"And then they kind of started their own sleazy rock kind of scene, because they were doing heroin and drinking and sleeping around with groupies for food, you know? And that was real. They weren't just doing it because it was cool—that's just who they were, and that's what separated Guns N' Roses from all those other bands.

"I don't think Guns N' Roses helped kill hair metal, but I think they did create a new avenue of escape for metal fans. I found myself coming back to metal through Guns N' Roses. Thanks to Guns N' Roses, I found that highway, because I was out seeing Jane's Addiction at Scream or the Music Machine or the Coconut Teazer, and Guns N' Roses is playing the Coconut Teazer and Guns N' Roses is playing the Music Machine. So they were kind of criss-crossing, you know? Guns N' Roses was playing areas the other glam bands weren't because they were a legitimate rock band. So they could play with Jane's

Addiction or they could play with the Chili Peppers, you know? But these other bands couldn't because they were stuck playing Gazzarri's with fifteen other hair bands that all sounded exactly the same.

"So Guns N' Roses did create an escape route, and it was a legitimate route that turned into a superhighway of rock. They were this monster band that cleaned house, created a new scene, revitalized hard rock again, made you realize that there's still a chance for hard rock and metal. And though they weren't technically a metal band—they were a hard rock band—they had elements of metal and metal kids connected with them. They were the first legitimate new LA band to show that it can still happen."

Neil Zlozower, photographer

"The glam scene was over when Guns N' Roses came out. There's pre-Guns and there's after Guns, okay? I did a very early Guns N' Roses shoot. They came in, and even though Axl had his hair poofed up for the first shoot, the second shoot was totally flat and straight. They came in and they still had the black leather coats and stuff, but you could see they didn't go to Ray Brown to get their clothes designed. I used to call them costumes. 'Hey guys, are you bringing your costumes?' 'Dude, they aren't costumes! They are our stage clothes.' 'Okay, sorry.' Before Guns, everybody was going to clothing designers and having stuff made, and pretty much after Guns, all the hair and hairspray started coming down. All the makeup got less and less, and all the clothing designers started to turn to ripped jeans and torn shirts and jean jackets. Even the Poison guys. I mean, I shot Danger Danger; they were all pretty boys one session, next session they had their Guns look.

"I mean, Guns N' Roses is a total success story. *Appetite for Destruction* is one of the all-time greatest rock records ever produced. It's very crude and raw, especially compared to *Use Your Illusion*. I mean, *Appetite* is just way up there. I think every single human being should have *Appetite for*

Ratt drummer Bobby Blotzer, during a stop on the *Invasion of Your Privacy* tour at the McMorran Arena in Port Huron, Michigan, July 18, 1985

Destruction in their record collection. But that bubble burst because of Guns and Metallica, who had a lot to do with it, too. Guns were still sort of the same music and genre as Mötley and everything. They're a little rougher, a little nastier, singing about, you know, shooting heroin. 'Mr. Brownstone,' 'It's So Easy'. . . I mean, the album is insane."

Barry Levine, photographer

"That whole hair metal thing, kids can tell if it's real, if it has balls, if it's going to sustain itself. And if it's not, they destroy it. I think that's what was happening. People were seeing that lyrically, most of these bands, outside of Guns N' Roses and Mötley Crüe, were singing about things that didn't really mean shit. They didn't have any substance."

Bobby Blotzer, Ratt

"I never felt any pressure. The only time I felt any sense of pressure, of 'Oh shit,' was when Guns N' Roses released their record. Because it was a badass record and a badass band. I was like, okay, we've got to keep on our toes here."

Alice in Chains, photographed at the Sheraton Airport Hotel, Los Angeles, September 14, 1990. Our muser on the Guns phenomenon, Sean Kinney, is pictured at far left.

Sean Kinney, Alice in Chains

"The main influence for me from that scene was Guns N' Roses, because they were more real and dangerous. *Appetite* is a great album and Duff is from Seattle. It kind of makes more sense to me. So, I think that's as far as I got into it. A lot of those songs hold up to the test of time. And our attitude seemed to be sort of like that, too. That was the band that stuck out the most for me. Style-wise, I tucked my pants in my cowboy boots for a minute [*laughs*]. There is a photo like that, and I think there was a spur on a Converse. You kind of had to piece together what you had. We were homeless guys, so whatever we could get or scam and do, you'd wear it. Yeah, trying to find your band's sound and identity is a natural process. Layne had a band with some of his friends that was called Alice in Chains but were like Guns N' Roses. They were a pretty hardcore kind of glam band, and as we'd taken that name, they had to move on."

Tawny Kitaen, a big part of Whitesnake's success through her appearance in the band's videos, pictured in Los Angeles, 1985

Tawny Kitaen, model and video star

"You know it's all Nirvana's fault, right? It's completely the success of Nirvana that killed rock 'n' roll. Guns N' Roses was like the only band that could really sustain itself in rock 'n' roll. All the rest of them, it was pretty much over. Game over for everyone except for Guns N' Roses."

we actually lived by. So, we took that aspect of it very seriously. Like if a song by any one of the bands that we were talking about had a great song that really spoke to us, genuinely spoke to us for a lot of different reasons, with the chord changes and the lyrics, it was really important. Whereas the bands that were around us at that time seemed to just be picking up on the surface stuff.

"I mean, Metallica is one of my favorite bands from that period. Bon Jovi was huge and Metallica was huge, and all of a sudden, we were getting pretty big. But we used to snicker at guys with the sort of Bon Jovi vibe. We were concentrating on what we were doing. We never had a camaraderie with any of those artists. And *Appetite for Destruction* is a cool record, but how it got to be as big as it was and still is to this day. . . . I mean, I couldn't tell you what the formula for that was. It was just us being us. Maybe in a different time, that same record might not have had the same impact."

Slash, in London, prior to performing at the *Freddie Mercury Tribute Concert* at Wembley Stadium.

ACT FOUR
ESTRANGED

4

26
YOU CAN'T PUT YOUR ARMS AROUND A MEMORY

Velvet Revolver and *Greatest Hits* dust-up

Velvet Revolver, left
to right: Slash, Scott
Weiland, Duff McKagan,
Matt Sorum, and Dave
Kushner, April 29, 2004.

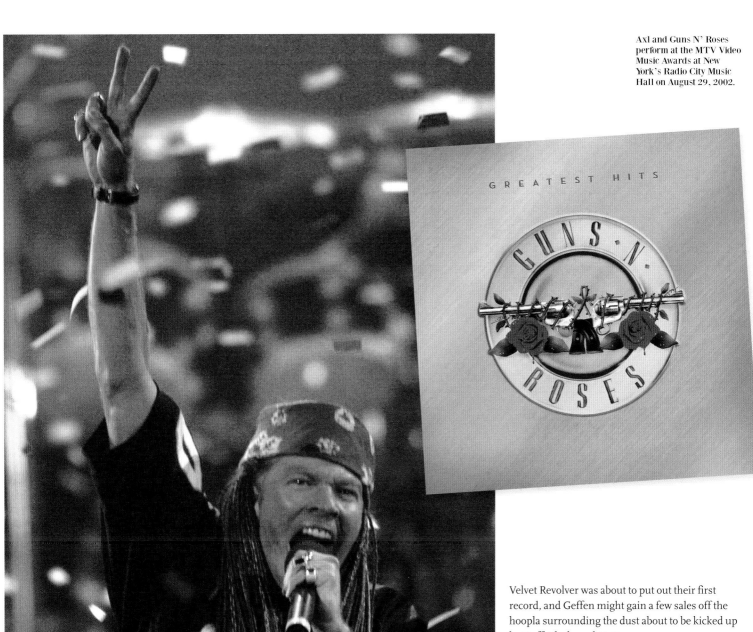

Axl and Guns N' Roses perform at the MTV Video Music Awards at New York's Radio City Music Hall on August 29, 2002.

GREATEST HITS

Rockers generally look at greatest-hits compilations negatively, arguably recalling how they themselves, as serious fans of bands when they were kids, considered hits packs for posers. Yet, sensibly, these albums tend to sell impressively, often becoming the biggest record in a band's catalog. And if the system works, everyone gets paid. But it's less fun when the band is broken up, as it is in this case, or more accurately, one party is running away with the brand. Axl had an extra reason to quash Geffen's

tabling of a hits record, namely that it would distract him and take focus away from finishing *Chinese Democracy*. The fact that it wasn't finished was part of the reason the label wanted it out in the first place, basically to feed the pipeline or otherwise keep the name in the public consciousness. They also were eager to recoup some of the money Axl was burning up on the long-delayed new album, in February 2004 telling Axl that they'd had enough and were suspending any further funding. Finally,

Velvet Revolver was about to put out their first record, and Geffen might gain a few sales off the hoopla surrounding the dust about to be kicked up by Duff, Slash, and Matt.

Axl, in fact, sued to stop the release, supported somewhat by both Slash and Duff, who recently also had been sued by the Guns management company and would soon be back on the offensive, filing a case against Axl in Los Angeles Superior Court five weeks after Geffen put *Greatest Hits* in the shops, March 23, 2004, having won the right to proceed. For Slash's part, he had nothing to do with the album. He was told what songs were on it and was at least relieved that they weren't attempting to remix the songs.

The album came wrapped in a simple silver digipak (mostly, regular jewel case in some territories) presentation emblazoned with a tasteful rendering of the band's logo and a title bereft of the nonsense applied to the live album (and many hits albums by other bands). But there was no liner essay, and just three pictures, one of Axl and Slash along with an overused band shot from the *Appetite* days, both in monochrome gray-and-white, plus a color CD tray inset shot. Bucking the chic corporate look of the thing is the fact that the CD is designed to looks like it's been angrily scratched past inoperable, which is ironic—or an in-joke—given the war over its issue.

That inevitably caused some fan distress, as did the track listing. The album starts out perfect, with "Welcome to the Jungle" and "Sweet Child o' Mine," both early songs and the band's biggest two hits. Next comes "Patience" from *GN'R Lies*, and then we're back to *Appetite* for "Paradise City." The following songs are all from *Use Your Illusion I* or *II*, and Geffen can't be faulted for any of these choices. The final three of the album's fourteen tracks are the most questionable. There are two from *"The Spaghetti Incident?"* and neither were a hit, not the bleak Dead Boys song and certainly not the '50s crooner tune, which seems to be stuck on there as punishment for being sued. Less offensive is the closing inclusion of the band's cover of "Sympathy of the Devil," which was indeed a moderate hit and had not appeared on an album yet. Then again, at nearly eight minutes and not particularly special, given a pointless break section and lots of jamming, it takes up precious space, not to mention that Slash was still pissed that Axl had added a Paul Huge guitar track on top of his guitar parts.

The illogical track sequence toward the album sent the signal that somebody didn't know what they were doing, underscoring the suspicion among fans that this was something put together without the full cooperation of the band. It also meant that there were five full covers on the album out of fourteen tracks, given that two pretty sensible choices were covers, namely "Knockin' on Heaven's Door" and "Live and Let Die." It also meant that there was no room for classic *Appetite* tracks like "It's So Easy," "Nightrain," "Out ta Get Me," "Rocket Queen," and "Mr. Brownstone." Plus, from the *Illusion* suite, folks are fond of "Double Talkin' Jive," "Pretty Tied Up," "Estranged," and "The Garden," all absent here as Geffen decides upon a single stuffed-full disc.

One wonders if part of the thinking on behalf of the label brass considered that *Appetite for Destruction* was a greatest-hits album all on its own, and that including everything substantive from it would compromise sales of that particular jewel in the Geffen crown. Even still, when Slash looked at the track list, he deemed it "way too obvious" and remarked that if he had his way, he would have done something more special with the release. Which is fair play. This could have been a double, with a book

The first ever Velvet Revolver press conference and show had the band performing at the El Rey Theatre in Los Angeles, June 19, 2003. They played two originals plus four other songs by the Sex Pistols, Nirvana, Stone Temple Pilots, and GN'R.

booklet, maybe some fancy merch inclusions, and maybe a reunion song or something, accompanied by full-press press.

Despite the absence of all that and minimal promotion, *Greatest Hits* sold vigorously, reaching #1 in a number of European territories (including the UK) and entering the Billboard charts at #3. It also reached #2 in Canada and #5 in Australia. A VH1 *Behind the Music* on the band, airing July 5, 2004, helped keep the chatter about the band going, and *Greatest Hits* was certified both gold and platinum on August 18, en route to its current five-times-platinum status, achieved at the last accounting back in 2011. A curious campaign for

the package took place in 2012, where, through a promotion between Amazon Music and Google Play, the digital version of the album was sold for one day at twenty-five cents. This caused the record to reenter the charts at #3, resulting in *Greatest Hits* becoming one of the top ten longest-charting albums of all time, at 631 weeks as of 2023.

Velvet Revolver at the Hard Rock Hotel & Casino, Hollywood, Florida, January 2, 2006

27
ABSURD
Izzy rejoins (sort of)

Izzy Stradlin guests with the Gunners as they headline day three of the Download Festival, Donington Park, United Kingdom, June 11, 2006.

Axl's world just gets weirder, beginning with his new and distinctive cornrow hairstyle and continuing on through with a clutch of warm-up gigs at the Hammerstein Ballroom in New York City for a new tour supporting a mirage of an album. There are celebrities galore, lavish parties, Sebastian Bach and his snorting chortle, and a fight with Tommy Hilfiger over the moving of a drink at an acoustic birthday party show. The band conduct shows on May 12, 14, and 15, 2006, but at the fourth and final show, on May 17, a reunion with Izzy Stradlin, for the first time since 1993, takes place, with Izzy playing on "Think About You," "Patience," and "Nightrain," the final selection also featuring Kid Rock. Elsewhere across the band's 140-minute

set, Sebastian helps Axl sing "My Michelle." Later, Axl is amused when Izzy says he's gotta get up early in the morning and then proceeds to skip out on the "Paradise City" encore and the epic after-party Axl has planned. Having grown up with him in Indiana, Axl knows what Izzy is like, and in fact, he's living a life just as surreal as Axl, except not completely revolving around rock 'n' roll.

Next comes the band's European tour, and although Izzy is not there for the first eight dates, he shows up for five shows in a row, from June 11 through June 20, with the first of Izzy's appearances being at the Download Festival in Donington. This time he plays on the same three songs he did in New York, along with "Used to Love Her" and "Paradise City." Izzy is there for shows in the Czech Republic, Poland, Austria, and France, before the band run into a postponement, because drummer Brain is about to be a dad and rushes home, to be replaced by Frank Ferrer, who is the band's drummer from then on to this very day. Frank's first show is on June 24 at Graspop Metal in Belgium, with Axl getting arrested three days after a scuffle with hotel security in Stockholm, Sweden. More dates ensue, with the band wrapping up performing two sold-out shows at Wembley Arena in London, where they surprise the crowd with some local songs, playing "Back in the USSR" by the Beatles, "Sailing" (which was covered and made into a hit by Rod Stewart), and "Sway" by the Rolling Stones—dates on this European tour supporting the Stones had to be canceled when Keith Richards fell out of a tree.

But by this point Izzy is long gone, back to his mystery life and back to his recent couple of very independent solo albums. He appears with the band again three times up into December and a few times in 2012, but he does not convert these magic cameos into a permanent position, either with the renegade Guns N' Roses swirled around *Chinese Democracy* or with the half-renegade configuration we enjoy to this day.

The reconstituted Guns N' Roses play at Gods of Metal in Milan, Italy, June 3 and 4, 2006.

28
PATIENCE

Dr Pepper linked to release of *Chinese Democracy*

Slash, who had just put out his autobiography, and the recently ousted Buckethead were exempt from the offer, but nonetheless on March 26, 2008, Dr Pepper promised everyone else in America a free can of pop if Guns N' Roses put out *Chinese Democracy* at any point within the current year.

As the press release quipped, "Dr Pepper is encouraging (ok, begging) Axl Rose to finally release his 17-year-in-the-making belabored masterpiece, *Chinese Democracy*, in 2008" and later "Dr Pepper supports Axl, and fully understands that sometimes you have to make it through the jungle before

you get it right." Drawing parallels, director of marketing for Dr Pepper, Jaxie Alt, mused, "It took a little patience to perfect Dr Pepper's special mix of twenty-three ingredients, which our fans have come to know and love. So we completely understand and empathize with Axl's quest for perfection."

Axl, appreciating the carbonated encouragement, issued a statement that read, "We are surprised and very happy to have the support of Dr Pepper with our album *Chinese Democracy* as for us this came totally out of the blue. If there is any involvement with this promotion by our record company or others, we are unaware of such at this time. And as some of Buckethead's performances are on our album I'll share my Dr Pepper with him." Slash found the promotion amusing as well, with Tommy Stinson relaying that if everybody in the country ponied up for their free Pepper, it would cost the company $180 million, which he described as a "hysterical footnote on the release of this record."

Also around this time, it was announced that the band was under new management, namely Irving Azoff and Andy Gould, replacing Merck Mercuriadis, who had left in December of the previous year. Meanwhile, Robin Finck was leaving the band for a second time, going back to Nine Inch Nails. Rumors had to be quashed that Axl might participate in a reality TV show based on the difficult birthing of *Chinese Democracy*.

When the album in fact did hit the shops in the fall of 2008 and it was time to pay up, the company's plan to distribute a downloadable coupon via their website fell to pieces, with their servers crashing. The one-day deadline was extended, but the system never quite recovered. This resulted in a souring of the promotion, with the band's lawyers firing off a letter of complaint and request for a full-page apology in the country's major newspapers as well as compensation, arguing that Dr Pepper was both taking advantage of the band's brand and now kind of damaging it, by fumbling the freebie. In the end, Axl put an end to the complaint, framing it as a nonissue, essentially, expressing the view that he had more important things to think about, like, for example, *Chinese Democracy*.

29
MR. BROWNSTONE
Steven records first episode of
Celebrity Rehab with Dr. Drew

Steven Adler plays with Adler's Appetite at a Key Club show commemorating the twentieth anniversary of *Appetite for Destruction*, Hollywood, California, July 28, 2007.

It's not just *Celebrity Rehab*, in which Steven Adler appeared over two seasons, the second and the fifth, or the *Sober House* spin-off show in 2009. No, there's something additional about his story that, logically, has kept the drummer in the news for years, but also has managed in some way to add to the legend of both Guns N' Roses and *Appetite for Destruction*. Essentially, this has been managed, at the negative end, by lurid headlines due to use of heavy drugs like cocaine and heroin, but also, on the positive, due to regular gigging and at least sporadic record-making, along with general availability to the public and the press. In other words, even though he's "just the drummer" and only on one-and-a-half Guns N' Roses albums, Steven is a bit of a B-celebrity, again, adding, through column inches and YouTube clips and regular stories at heavy metal websites like our own BraveWords.com, to the legend of this band and its perennial pirate escapades, not that Guns N' Roses is ever lacking for attention.

Even before his ouster for the band, Steven busted up his hand punching a streetlight, resulting in Fred Coury from Cinderella being brought in to replace him over several shows on a tour with Alice Cooper. Indeed, on top of doing the most drugs, Steven was the band's designated brawler. Then Don Henley had to step in for an *American Music Awards* show while Steven tried one of his many stints in rehab. Threatened with firing, as discussed, Steven was forced to sign a contract avowing that he'd get off drugs, but then things got even worse, with Steven missing rehearsals, holing up in a house, and basically cutting off much contact with the guys. He finally was let go on July 11, 1990, and what followed was an audition for AC/DC (scotched by public warnings from Axl), a reformation of Road Crew, lawsuits over publishing with his former bandmates, and a 1995 arrest for heroin possession. Then there was the 1996 speedball-induced coma and stroke that permanently damaged his ability to speak.

But as alluded to, some music got made as well, and Steven remained part of the Guns N' Roses narrative, for better or worse. There was a stint with BulletBoys, once a promising baby version of Van Halen and now just an old hair band trying to get by with a compromised lineup. In 2003, we got Steven's *Appetite* and again, there's that name on the marquee, along with an association with what was by far Steven's resumé highlight. In the press, from Steven's low-rent end of the business, discussion was kept alive about the golden era of Guns, significantly because this band was playing much of the first album in their sets, along with songs by Led Zeppelin and Aerosmith, tacitly proposing that there's an arc toward *Appetite* that begins with top-tier greatness from the '70s. Heck, even Slash and Izzy joined the band onstage, back in September 2003 at the Key Club in Hollywood, running through renditions of "Mr. Brownstone," "Paradise City," and "Knockin' on Heaven's Door." In 2007, it was Izzy showing up again but with Duff this time, the two ex-combatants jumping onstage with Steven's band, who had been busy celebrating the twentieth anniversary of *Appetite for Destruction*.

Then, on October 23, 2008, Steven appeared for the first time on *Celebrity Rehab with Dr. Drew* and his legend multiplied. Perhaps that's overstating it, but it was indeed a comparatively modest but still significant version of the mainstream penetration old rockers like Gene Simmons and Ozzy Osbourne enjoyed with their hit runs on reality TV, not to mention Bret Michaels and Vince Neil. Across seasons two and five, Steven appeared as the sort of cautionary tale told on many a GN'R song, and he'd do the same on season one of *Sober House*. The guy came out sufficiently humanized, and he became certainly more familiar to mainstream pop culture than Axl or Izzy. One supposes that the gulf would be less compared to Duff and Slash, who have been gracious and available and amiable members of rock 'n'

Above: Steven, Duff, and Izzy backstage at the Key Club event

Left: Road Crew—Davy Vain, Steven Adler, Ashley Mitchell, Jamie Scott, and Shawn Rorie—in Los Angeles in 1992

roller culture for many years now, rehabilitated and friends of all of us, to some extent. But still, it's weird that we know so much about the drummer on one Guns N' Roses album.

Steven remained in the public eye over the ensuing years, again, continuing to put the name Guns N' Roses in the news, in a variety of ways. First, Slash had him on a track on his *Slash* solo album from 2010. There were continuing revolving lineups of Steven's *Appetite*, but also, in 2012, the man's only full-length album since the first Guns N' Roses record came out, credited to band name Steven and called *Back from the Dead*. There's a track on the album called "Just Don't Ask" and who is playing on it but Steven's old Road Crew buddy Slash?

Also that year, despite the drama and trauma caused to a band that were no angels themselves, Steven was included as part of Guns N' Roses' Rock & Roll Hall of Fame induction (unfortunately this was followed in 2013 by more struggles with sobriety). But then on July 6, 2016, Steven guested at a GN'R show in Cincinnati, rocking his way through renditions of "Out ta Get Me" and "My Michelle." Further cameo appearances took place in Nashville, Buenos Aires, and hometown LA, and, through such demonstrations of largess, it appeared that the band had let bygones be bygones.

Jamming onstage at the Key Club anniversary show, left to right: Izzy Stradlin, Chip Znuff from Enuff Znuff, Duff, Steven, Colby Veil, and Michael Thomas.

30
14 YEARS
GN'R releases *Chinese Democracy*

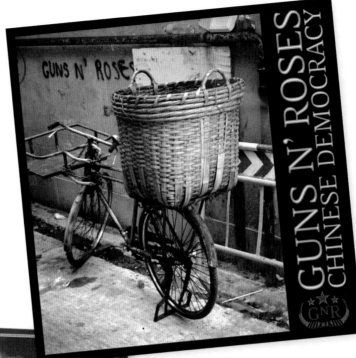

"A work of art is never finished, merely abandoned." That idea, in more words than that and in French, is attributed to Paul Valéry from an essay he wrote back in 1933. It's a famous quote because it's a good one, and according to Tommy Stinson, Axl was still wanting to fix a few things (mostly in the art department) when Geffen snatched *Chinese Democracy* from his hands and prepared it for public consumption. The old Guns-adjacent title track was already available as an advance single, "Shackler's Revenge" had shown up in a video game, and "If the World" was in a movie, but on November 23, 2008, the entirety of the sweeping new Guns N' Roses album entered the physical realm, through an exclusive deal with Best Buy. It answered all sorts of questions, most pointedly and poignantly who Axl was as an artist and as a person.

His pronouncements on the record upon release were both thoughtful and inspiring. He saw *Chinese Democracy* as a positive album defiantly thrust into a world with plenty of negativity and other effects threatening to damage fragile psyches. He also recognized that it was an album well beyond the blues rock boundaries of the old band, and he refused to worry about how heavy metal it was. Perceptively, he, as well as Buckethead, eloquently talked about how much it was an album that guitarists could appreciate. And they are right on that front—one can put headphones on and try to discern the brainwork put into the arranging and layering of rhythm parts, or one can just rock out and wait, air guitar in hand, for the next surprising, creative, clean, or effects-laden solo passage. It's also a vocal showcase, with Axl often singing clean and high, stacking parts, showing thespian versatility, and generally exploring this corner of the rubber room as much as all the other areas of dense detailing that make *Chinese Democracy* a challenging listen.

The album opens with a minute of foreboding Pink Floyd–like sound effects, but then we're into the title track, which sounds like punk rockin' ol' Gunners, with Axl scowling his way through a double-tracked lead vocal that sounds straight out of 1991. But there are also subtly massaged-in layers of electronics, and political lyrics inspired by the three months Axl spent in China. Predictably, China's Communist regime came out and banned the album based on this pro-democracy song flagged for scrutiny by its title and the title of the whole damn album.

With "Shackler's Revenge," we get to see Axl's appreciation for modern metal. It's essentially a "spookycore" Coal Chamber–type song, atonal, industrial, screechy, with Axl injecting into the cacophony a lower-register monotone vocal, a suitable choice for a song inspired by the senselessness of school shootings. Still, there's melody, a strong, linear pre-chorus, and memorable chorus, as well as stomping real drums.

"Better," excepting the shopping trip-hop intro, is a darling slice of hard alternative, with an exquisite vocal melody at the pre-chorus and then a tribal, thrusting chorus that reminds one of Skid Row. There's sweep-picking and then comes the break. Over stomping new heavy metal music, there's a wah-wah solo that has turned out to be one of Axl's favorite parts of the album. Next is "Street of Dreams," a sturdy, powerful ballad driven by drums and piano, but still, upholding the theme of the record, blessed with heroic guitar parts and a daunting, expressive Axl, as gritty as he ever gets and then almost disconcertingly clean, while a string arrangement carries on in the background (although one complaint about this record is that there's so much going on, we lose a sense of foreground and background).

It's interesting that keyboardist Chris Pittman, prime mover of "If the World," describes this song using terms like "funk," "dub," and "reggae," whereas Axl is thinking James Bond and

Axl and Ron "Bumblefoot" Thal at the Roskilde Festival in Roskilde, Denmark, June 29, 2006

Buckethead performs with Guns N' Roses at the MTV Video Music Awards, Radio City Music Hall, New York City, August 29, 2002.

blaxploitation films. In the end, it's a shocking outlier, a bridge too far for many, but even if one rejects the premise, one can revel in the top-shelf vocals and also the tone, taste, and tenacity of the guitar parts. "There Was a Time" is another orchestrated ballad but with stadium rock drums. Axl's vocal gets a slight electronic effect, but it's impossible to ponder what's going on with his singing for too long, because there are so many instruments to check out in the arrangement, not to mention surprise chord changes. "Catcher in the Rye" is another ballad—about the confluence of John Lennon, Mark David Chapman, and *The Catcher in the Rye*—and one is instantly taken back to Axl's stated aim of bringing more beauty into Guns N' Roses, somehow locating hope or healing in the lyrics, the light shining through Beatle-esque and Queen-like. Speaking of Queen, a bit of a diplomatic kerfuffle occurred when Brian May himself recorded a solo for the song and Axl ended up not using it.

"Scraped," from Buckethead, begins with orchestrated a capella vocals, but quickly we're into a percussive, alternative heavy metal thing that reminds us how much of a fan Axl was of Jane's Addiction. So much is happening though, with complex, stratified vocals and also singing over guitar solos, which, negatively speaking, might sound belabored. Conversely, however, it floats the idea that there's perhaps intentionally something like an album's worth of information in every song, which makes for a worthy artistic concept to be embraced or at least debated in good faith.

"Riad N' the Bedouins" amusingly combines Jane's Addiction (or Soundgarden) with typical, expected, marauding Guns N' Roses tropes, despite its fancy-pants title and lyrics that are possibly about the Iraq War and international arms sales, supposedly the occupation of a relative to Axl by marriage, back when he was with Erin Everly. An incidental part of the intro caused a copyright dispute and then lawsuit, adding to the unceasing flood of drama associated with this almost Keystone Kops version of the band. "Sorry" is a despondent but passion-filled blues ballad performed at an extremely slow tempo. But again, upholding the narrative of the album, soon we get huge guitars and squalling Tony Iommi–like wah-wah burbling, not to mention David Gilmour and Stevie Ray Vaughn–like licks that build to a frightening crescendo and then spacey fade.

Next, "I.R.S." is further proof that Axl has built something special here. There's a direct link with the guitar hero power chords back to *Use Your Illusion*, but then there are unexpected chord changes, electronic passages, and enigmatic lyrics that speak to intense experiences and emotions that could only come from the crazy—and privileged—life of Axl. Or you could listen to it just for the variously shredding and sighing guitar solos.

"Madagascar" features bits of dialogue from a bunch of movies as well as from speeches by Martin Luther King Jr. But at the music's end, despite orchestration and a part-time hip-hop beat, it's pretty conventional, taking us back to "Don't Cry," "Civil War," Knockin' on Heaven's Door," and "November Rain." More shocking is "This I Love," an ornate and classical piano ballad well suited to a Broadway play. True to *Chinese Democracy* norms,

there's a prominent, scorching guitar solo, Brian May–like, and then we're back into Axl's torrid vocal and lyric concerning a past lost love. This one actually had been recorded back during the *Use Your Illusion* sessions but obviously didn't make the cut. Axl has called the orchestral arrangement on the bridge section of "This I Love" his favorite part of the whole album.

The album closes with "Prostitute," which is much more epic than its street-level title would suggest. The song almost serves as a microcosm for the album as a whole, revisiting the record's regularly addressed synthesis of hard rock and modern beats, while layering in quite classical orchestration just to include more from Axl's complex bag of tricks and tropes. Playing to the newly raised sense of expectation, nurtured over the course of this ambitious and creatively triumphant album, "Prostitute" ends in dramatic fashion, violent and guitar-strafed and then classical but subdued, drawn gracefully to a close, nearly the last third of the song's six minutes drawing us down.

All told, as Axl regularly reminds us, it's all about the art, and if it takes a long time to get there, so be it. But it seems like the record-breaking wait for *Chinese Democracy*—by some measures seventeen years and by others a dozen—had resulted in a general sense of various factions being over it before it could begin. Many of the songs had been leaked early and the knives were coming out, because, really, what record could possibly live up to this much anticipation? Critics spent more time talking about the drama in the band than the songs, as did fans. When they did address the album, they framed it as overblown, overworked, overproduced, and overlong. On the overlong front, one might look at the fact that there are fourteen songs on the album that exist within a tight range between 3:30 and 6:40, but mostly around five minutes, a duration that often causes one to think that

what we have here is a regular four-minute song with a minute of filler, in other words, a bloated song. But as we've seen, that's not really the case. If anything, one might look at some of these as abbreviated versions of progressive rock songs or songs like "November Rain" and "Estranged"—compressed so that Axl can shoehorn in all the ideas that have been filling his head all these building-to-burst years.

When asked about the album, Matt Sorum was devastating in his silence and Duff seemed to be mostly complimentary about Axl's singing. Slash, on the other hand, seemed very pleased with it, accurately remarking that this was where Axl was heading as an artist when they parted, and that it was a great record that he couldn't have possibly gotten out of the original band.

Black clouds intensifying, Axl and his new manager, Irving Azoff, were suing each other, Azoff complaining about perceived financial improprieties and Axl complaining that management had undermined the success of the album. Axl's suspicions were that the record label wanted the album to fail to trigger a reunion with the old band, and that as a result, Interscope did very little to promote the album. In alignment with that, Axl blamed Azoff for the song leaks, the unimpressive cover art, and the less-than-ideal arrangement with Best Buy for exclusive physical sales.

In the end, despite the sneers and howls, *Chinese Democracy* sold commendably, given how 2008 was in and around the end of the road for the dominance of physical CD sales, with vinyl a pittance. First week numbers of 261,000 were considered a disappointment, as was the fact that in 2011, Best Buy had to clear out their remaining stock—they'd bought 1.3 million unreturnable copies at about $10.77 a pop—for the embarrassing price of $2. Still, the album certified platinum within a year, reaching that plateau in many countries around the world and even triple platinum in Canada. It's currently sold about three million copies worldwide.

Axl Rose in victory pose
at the Continental Airlines
Arena, Rutherford, New
Jersey, November 5, 2006

31
MY WORLD
GN'R embarks on first *Chinese Democracy* tour

Curious and enigmatic as always, Guns N' Roses issued *Chinese Democracy* in March 2008 but didn't begin touring for it until December 11 , 2009. They played seven songs from the "new" album on their first date, and then actually all but one—thirteen songs, excepting "Riad N' the Bedouins"—at the Tokyo show on December 19, the last of a four-night Far East stand. This date, at the Tokyo Dome, turned out to be the band's longest show ever, at three hours and thirty-seven minutes. Axl was clearly proud of the album and eager to deliver these songs now that they were finally hitting the road, almost two-and-a-half years since their last date, back in July 2007 in Osaka, Japan. Interestingly, in 2007, they already were somewhat touring *Chinese Democracy*, delivering "Better," "Street of Dreams," and "I.R.S." and then up into the encore, "Chinese Democracy" and "Madagascar."

GN'R's touring lineup for these dates (and beyond into Canada in mid-January) included a substantial amount of the players who wrote and performed on the now year-and-a-half-old record. And it's a juggernaut: Axl had with him three guitarists, namely Bumblefoot, Richard Fortus, and DJ Ashba, and two keyboardists, Dizzy Reed and Chris Pitman. On bass was Tommy Stinson and on drums was Frank Ferrer. From that lot, only DJ Ashba, from Indiana like Axl and Izzy, was new, replacing Robin Finck. Ashba had been a well-traveled veteran of the scene by this point, having played with Bulletboys, Beautiful Creatures, and Sixx:A.M., alongside Nikki Sixx. Ashba would be a Gunner for the next five years before resuming Sixx:A.M. duties. By this point, all the wars with manager Irving Azoff had come to a head and the band was doing all this without a manager.

After the extensive coast-to-coast Canadian campaign, the band spent March into early April in South America, then went to Central America, and then over to Europe, beginning May 31, 2010, in Norway. Nipping back to play the Sturgis bike fest, the band was then back to Europe for a blanketing of the continent from late August through October 23, in Barcelona, Spain. It must be said that the legend of Axl and the strange career path he'd been embarking on all these years, kept curiosity levels high, with full arenas everywhere, although in Canada, venues were mostly the smaller B-city hockey barns. Next it was over to Australia in December 2010, with the band closing out the year with a single show in Abu Dhabi.

Ten months passed before the band resumed their surreal prerelease and very post-release *Chinese Democracy* campaign, returning to South America, where Guns N' Roses mania never waned. Finally, beginning in late October, America finally got its due, with the band playing intensively through to the end of the year. But representing that something was afoot, Duff began a handful of serial cameos, with the first being at the O2 Arena in London, October 14, 2010, where he joined the band for "You Could Be Mine," Knockin' on Heaven's Door," "Nice Boys," and "Patience."

This page and opposite:
Chinese Democracy tour,
County Stadium, Taipei,
Taiwan, December 11, 2009

32
YOU COULD BE MINE
The Up Close and Personal tour

Shaking things up not because he has to but because being a performance artist is just an extra way of being an artist, Axl decided to conduct a campaign of smaller venues in the States. The Up Close and Personal tour consisted essentially of theaters and large clubs, but the guys still played long, dramatic shows like they were in arenas and stadiums, just with less actual fire. The idea speaks to the same creative motivations that might have found Axl leaving a show early or showing up for one late, namely the search for the perfect magical way to deliver the songs. Again, there's a performance art or contemporary art component, and also an adherence to the narrative that one should expect something surreal when experiencing Guns N' Roses—I suspect if someone would have suggested a tour of venues with a capacity of one seat, Axl would chuckle and not dismiss it out of hand.

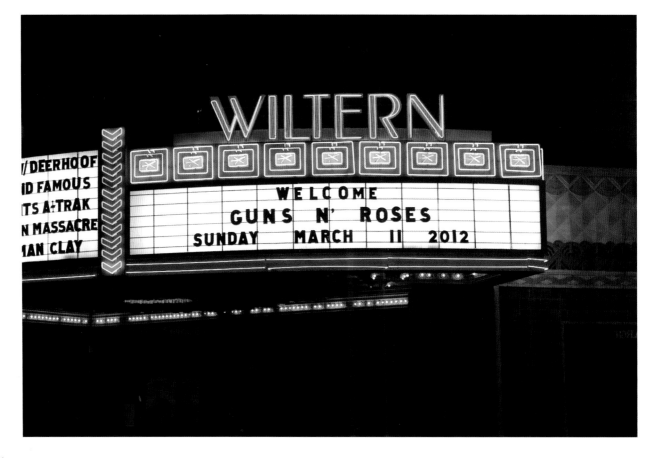

Axl and guitarist DJ Ashba
at the Wiltern show in Los
Angeles, March 11, 2012

Inspiringly, the band was the same eight-headed monster that toured the previous year, proving that if you could keep up with Axl, you were a Gunner. Bumblefoot, however, was on a nerve-blocker for back pain due to a car accident, so he was compromised, with the situation most grave at the Electric Factory in Philadelphia, where he repeatedly had to leave the stage. DJ Ashba talked about the excitement and responsibility he had delivering to what he perceived as the most dedicated of Guns fans, given the limited tickets, and Dizzy talked about how he was closer to the front of the stage and felt more integrated into the band.

There were eight shows in a city at the middle of the tour, but to begin it, New York City saw four shows in four different venues, February 10 through 16, and to end it, Los Angeles saw three shows in three different venues, March 9 through March 12. The disorienting array of acts supporting the Gunners at these shows—Handsome Dick Manitoba, Chelsea Smiles, Toilet Boys, Electric Sun, Sponge, the Last Vegas, Fall of Envy, Bob Lee Rodgers, Falling in Reverse, and Goldsboro— also speaks to the sort of enthusiastic musical education Axl was suggesting with the radicalized Guns lineup.

After the US run, the concept loosened and the band headed off to Europe, May 11 to July 1, followed by a single show in Tel Aviv, Israel, and a short campaign in Eastern Europe. Added with the sprawling touring the band had done since 2001, Guns N' Roses now had quietly built themselves into a global band, willing world travelers, with the tacit messaging being that audiences outside of the United States are more amenable to change.

Peppered through the campaign, the band did a modicum of press, with the subject of new music coming up regularly. The impression was that the band was limiting its live work so that they could get back to the many demos they had been doing toward the release of a follow-up to *Chinese Democracy*. For his part, Bumblefoot tried to impose some order by suggesting the band write and record one song before every touring leg, and then release it as a single and play the new song live. Little did they know that despite many more dates in 2012, 2013, and 2014, celebrating twenty-five years since *Appetite for Destruction*, the "performance art" years would draw to a close, with no more music to show for it, other than *Chinese Democracy*, hefty and left-handed, quite singular, and still one of only four Guns N' Roses records proper.

This page and opposite: Green Day inducted Guns N' Roses into the Rock & Roll Hall of Fame on December 7, 2011. Below, Green Day guitarist and vocalist Billie Joe Armstrong presents a Hall statuette to Duff.

33
KNOCKIN' ON HEAVEN'S DOOR
Induction into the Rock & Roll Hall of Fame

We expected them to bring some drama, and they didn't disappoint. As soon as Guns N' Roses were nominated for induction into the Rock & Roll Hall of Fame on December 7, 2011, the chattering classes began speculating who would be tapped on the shoulder for inclusion and who would show up to accept, not to mention if there would be a performance and who would take part. All those questions were answered when on April 14, 2012, all of Green Day took the stage to induct the band, who got in about ten years after first becoming eligible. The ceremony in Cleveland included induction for Beastie Boys, Donovan, Laura Nyro, Red Hot Chili Peppers, and the Small Faces/Faces, making for a ragtag bunch relatively low on wattage this time 'round.

Billie's speech started perfunctory, reading from the page, head down, but he quickly got into it and began ad-libbing. He also personalized it by saying he bought *Appetite for Destruction* (assumingly back in the day) and that it was "the best debut album in the history of rock 'n' roll." He also called Steve Adler's drumming perfect and called Duff "Johnny Thunders with a bass." He also extoled the virtues of Izzy Stradlin's "Ronnie Wood mojo." At that point,

cameras moved to a shot of Ronnie himself, there to get inducted as part of the Faces. Billie called out Dizzy Reed and Matt Sorum too, and then called Slash a cross between Eric Clapton, Jimmy Page, and Joe Perry, but with a modern twist. Next, Billie had to quiet the boos of the crowd when it came time to say something nice about Axl, absent from the proceedings.

After Billie's ultimately kind of goofy speech, ambling onto the stage were Duff, Slash, and a pair of drummers, Matt Sorum and Steven Adler, which was good to see, because both deserved to be inducted. As alluded to, Axl stayed away, musing in a public statement, "So let sleeping dogs lie or lying dogs sleep or whatever. Time to move on. People get divorced. Life doesn't owe you your own personal happy ending especially at another's, or in this case several others', expense." The reclusive Izzy Stradlin also demurred, writing, "I have waited up to this point to see what would become of the GN'R induction into Rock & Roll Hall of Fame. I would like to say THANK YOU and GRACIAS to Rock & Roll Hall of Fame for the acknowledgment of our works over the years as a band. BIG THANKS to all my bandmates who helped get us to where we are today."

First to the microphone was Duff, who remarked (without notes) that after the guys first met "in the rank back alleys in Hollywood" and became a band, they "created brutality and beauty and told the truth all at once but we were writing these songs for ourselves." He also said that "I don't know if it matters who's here tonight because it's about the music that that band created." Next was a beaming Steven, who introduced himself by saying, "I play drums and the cowbell." He then quoted Freddie Mercury from "We Are the Champions," thanked everybody, and ceded the platform to Slash, who thanked the fans and his wife, who evidently talked Slash into coming to the ceremony. Amusingly, he called Guns N' Roses "the band that was born to lose that actually made it." Finally, we got Matt, who told the story of living at home and his mom taking a call from Slash to ask if he'd join the band. Also, commenting on Slash's speech, he said, "That's more than I've ever heard Slash talk in his entire life."

The performance segment of the show kicked off with "Mr. Brownstone," and onstage were new Hall of Famers Duff, Slash, and Matt, along with Gilby Clarke, who I'd say appropriately was left out

of the induction, and Myles Kennedy from Slash's band at the all-important vocal spot. There was a moment of panic when the guys plugged into the standard provided backline, and Clarke's amp suddenly started smoking. There were no techs on hand and only three Marshall heads and Slash had one of the other two. Fortunately, the last one worked, and a guitar sound was sorted out while Matt executed the song's opening jungle drumbeat.

Next came "Sweet Child o' Mine," with Steven now at the drums, followed by an awkward but perfunctory introduction of Gilby. The band lit into "Paradise City" and Matt gamely reappeared, positioned next to Gilby and whacking a tambourine. Steven played awesome, and after a nice fill at the close of the song, Matt jumped up on the drum riser in what looked like surprise and admiration.

Also doing a bang-up job was Kennedy, who capably steered his way through Axl's many modes and moods on the three classic *Appetite* tracks, expected from Slash's right-hand man and one of the top consummate pros on the classic rock circuit. What's more, he struck the right tone for the evening, not vamping and stealing the spotlight, making sure the focus stayed on Duff and Slash and these songs so perfectly and soberly played.

The band's Hall of Fame performance featured Myles Kennedy from Slash's band on vocals, along with Duff, Slash, and Matt Sorum, who shared the stage with Steven Adler (inset).

Loose Ends

CHINESE DEMOCRACY PROGRESS REPORT

Axl and Tommy Stinson,
O2 Arena, London,
October 13, 2010

Back on September 10, 2004, I had a hotel interview with Tommy Stinson about his solo album, *Village Gorilla Head*. But I also asked him about his experience with Guns N' Roses, and here are those excerpts. Little did either of us know that *Chinese Democracy* was still four years away at that point.

Popoff: Are there any tracks on *Village Gorilla Head* that were potential GN'R tracks or, going way back, potential Replacements tracks?

Stinson: No, no. I mean, I've always given my stuff to Axl to see if there's anything on there that maybe he would want to throw on a GN'R record, and he listened to these, but I think by the time he heard these, most of the GN'R record was pretty much done. But out of courtesy, because he's been very supportive of me, I give him stuff to see. Maybe there's something that he had to have, or something like that. But that not being the case, none of them were really meant to be GN'R songs.

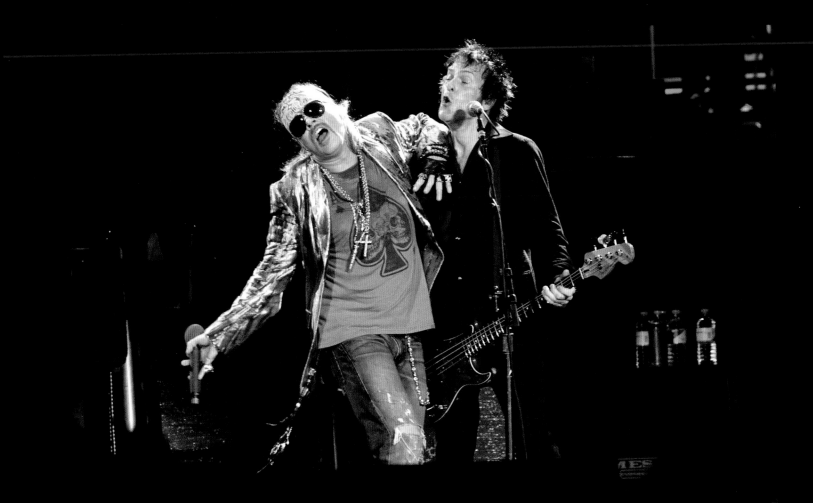

Frank Ferrer channels his inner Jason Bonham at the Wiltern, Los Angeles, March 11, 2012

Axl and guitarist Richard
Fortus at the Mediolanum
Forum of Assago in Milan,
Italy, September 5, 2010

Popoff: What are your contributions to the GN'R record?

Stinson: Well, I think pretty much all of us in the band have some songwriting credits on just about everything. The undertaking was pretty much a large collaboration between eight people, even a couple others who aren't around anymore, but maybe started with pieces of the old band or whatever. But yeah, there is probably a lot to go around with that one.

Popoff: Where is the album going stylistically?

Stinson: Stylistically speaking, if I were to take a stab at it, it would probably be something more focused than *Use Your Illusion*. I think *Use Your Illusion* was going in a couple of other musical directions a little bit, but not fully realized. I think there were some limitations to where the band was maybe willing to go? That has been taken out of the mix.

Popoff: So it's more focused, you say?!

Stinson: More focused, but also more diverse. I think the music on the new GN'R record will be a lot more complex, a little more far-reaching, probably, in a lot of ways? As well as there will be some rock there that will be reminiscent of the older records. But for the most part, stylistically speaking, there's a lot more going on. And I would say lyrically, definitely there is a lot more going on versus the old Guns. There's a lot more introspection, a lot more social commentary involved.

Popoff: Are the lyrics all Axl, or are you guys in on them, too?

Stinson: No, most of the lyrics are all Axl.

Popoff: Do you keep regular hours?

Stinson: I try, but it doesn't work out a lot of the time [*laughs*]. With all the different little commitments and things going on.

Popoff: How about with GN'R? Do you guys try to keep regular hours? Does Axl keep regular hours?

Stinson: We try. Axl is a strange cat in that his biological clock runs on a 36-hour day, as opposed to 24-hour day. It's a very odd thing, but it's very real. Not like accurately, but it's like, he needs more of the day than there is. And it's not because of any sort of fault or anything; it's just that that is how his body works. And I've only met a few people like that in my life, and he's one of them [*laughs*].

Popoff: Who are the main contributors on what will ultimately be *Chinese Democracy*?

Stinson: There'll probably be compositions that started with each of us and were compiled by all of us on the whole record, yeah. I would be willing to wager that that is how it turns out, because Axl is the kind of guy who is always looking out for the fairest way to do it so everyone's happy. Because obviously, that's the kind of thing that screwed up the old band. Everybody had songs they wanted to write, and have Axl sing, and then there got to be infighting, I think, with whose songs were going to be on the record and things like that. He's really conscious of that, so it ends up being a bit of everyone on there.

Popoff: Does everyone sing on it?

Stinson: I think Dizzy and I sing on it a lot. Dizzy and I came up with a good amount of background vocal parts and different things like that, but mostly him and I are the background singers.

Popoff: Now, will you tour this solo album, *Village Gorilla Head*? I mean, where does this fit in with GN'R tour plans?

Stinson: It fits into the GN'R plan. When there is downtime between tours, I might do some one-offs or short runs to support that record. That's kind of what I envision. I don't know. Until I get into the thick of the GN'R thing, I'm pretty sure that when the record comes out, we'll be on the road for the next year and a half or so. And there will be some big breaks in there when I go out and do my own thing.

Popoff: Does Axl have any insecurities about putting out this record with respect to fulfilling expectations?

Stinson: Oh, I'm sure. With any undertaking of that nature, where you've got so much riding on it, but also when you have so much expectation weighing on you, I'm sure it's gotta weigh on him a little bit. We don't really talk about it much, because I don't really want to talk about it and make him think about it if he's not thinking about it, you know what I mean? But I think more than that weighing on him is that he wants to be sure that he's gotten his points across and gotten it the way he envisions it. And I think we've gotten down to the very final elements of it where I listened to some of the final mixes to it before I left LA, to just get my two cents in on it, because it will probably go to master while I'm gone.

Popoff: Will it be out in October?

Stinson: Oh, I would imagine they would start mastering it sometime in October, November, somewhere in there. I just wanted to make sure I got my two cents in so I couldn't look back and go, "Dudes, what's up?" And they go, "Dude, where were you? You didn't say anything!" So I got my two cents in on it.

Popoff: And what was your two cents?

Stinson: Oh, my two cents was very much like a cent and a half. It's like, all the stuff I heard was phenomenal. I didn't get a chance to listen to all of it, because I was pressed for time. But also, I wanted to hear the things I hadn't heard yet. Some of the stuff had been done a while ago and hadn't changed much; I didn't really bother with that. But I wanted to hear all the new stuff, and I heard about six things that I hadn't really heard finished yet that were really mind-blowing.

Popoff: Is it a really long album?

Stinson: A few of the songs are pretty epic in length, but that's always been GN'R's thing, hasn't it? I don't think it's a particularly long album, but I think the six I heard are pretty epic. I mean they are just fucking huge, you know? [*laughs*].

Popoff: How about a little psychological profile of Axl? What are his strengths, his weaknesses?

Stinson: Wow. I would say his strengths are definitely his heart and his loyalties. He's incredibly loyal and totally has your back if you're straight with him and are loyal back. Which is why him and I have gotten along so well. I'm the same sort of person. I don't fuck around or waste my time with people who waste my time, and I don't really take up people's time if they don't want it. I would say those are his strengths. Other than that, he's a fucking awesome singer and an amazing songwriter. Other than that, the weaknesses part? Maybe he still thinks too much of what people are expecting of him. Maybe he thinks about it a little too much. Maybe he could try just fucking exist, and not worry about the way people want him to be. Maybe a little bit of that? Might be hard for him, because he's got a lot riding on it. I've got a lot riding on it, but he's obviously got *way* more [*laughs*].

Popoff: Have you seen in that situation just some crazy business stuff? Where it just makes you shake your head? Like crazy things people ask you to do?

Stinson: No, nothing like that, really. More what I see with the Guns N' Roses thing is just that there's . . . you know, I've hung out with him so much to know that it's hard to be him, just because people are rabid. They get pretty weirded-out. He's got some crazy fans, and people that have been there for a long time. And I think if he could just exist, if he could get up in the day and go cruise around like I cruise around and see the world in a non-stressful environment like that [*laughs*], it might do some good for his fuckin' . . . his self. He's a huge fucking rock star, man. He can barely go down the street without someone fuckin' throwing some curveball at him. It's a bummer.

Axl and Bumblefoot in Milan, September 5, 2010

ACT FIVE
LEGACY

34
DON'T DAMN ME
The first reunion-era tour

Axl and Slash reunited,
Soldier Field, Chicago,
July 3, 2016

The chain of events that led to a Guns N' Roses reunion tour, which became the fourth biggest grossing rock 'n' roll campaign of all time, begins, in fact, with J Ashba, Bumblefoot, and Tommy Stinson all leaving the band. Concurrently, Slash had been making statements that the tension that he had once had with Axl had "dissipated," and that a reunion tour "for the right reasons" would be good for the fans. But Andrew Dice Clay also deserves some credit for the patching up of relations, talking to both Axl and Slash on different occasions, encouraging them to get together, as did Steven Tyler.

At the drum end, neither Steven Adler nor Matt Sorum would make the grade and Izzy Stradlin declined to be involved, stating that "they didn't want to split the loot equally." Overtures were definitely sent Izzy's way, with the guys inviting him to rehearsals where his amps were all ready to go; however, week after week, he never showed up. Previous GN'R manager Alan Niven commented that without Izzy and Steven, the lineup lacked legitimacy. As the reunion began to take shape, DJ Ashba was

checked in on again, but confirmed that he was going to sit it out, wishing to concentrate in Sixx:A.M.

As for keyboards, Chris Pitman, who saw the whole thing as a money grab and said as much on Twitter, was on the outs, to be replaced by Brain's writing partner Melissa Reese, who would be responsible for keyboards, sub-bass tones, synths, some of the *Chinese Democracy* samples, and backing vocals. She remains part of the band to this day. This left from the renegade band guitarist Richard Fortus and drummer Frank Ferrer, who indeed would be part of the densely populated juggernaut that was Guns N' Roses 3.0.

The January 5, 2016, press release to make the situation official read, in part, as follows: "Upholding a three-decade tradition of breaking ground, creating trends, and forever changing the face of rock 'n' roll, Guns N' Roses announce the most significant and anxiously awaited musical event of this century. Founder Axl Rose and former members Slash and Duff McKagan will regroup to headline the Coachella Music &

The band takes a bow at Dodger Stadium in Los Angeles, August 19, 2016. This was the second of two nights, with the Cult supporting.

Soldier Field, Chicago, July 3, 2016

Arts Festival (April 15–17 and April 22–24). For months, critics and audiences alike have generated immense excitement and speculation over the possible regrouping of the iconic lineup. The April performances will mark the first time since 1993 the Gunners will share the stage for what is certain to be an explosive event."

The wording was kept vague because it hadn't been determined at that point just who else would be part of the band, with Velvet Revolver's Dave Kushner being rumored to be part of the conversation. There was a chance Steven Adler would be the drummer as well, but then he injured his back at the worst possible time, when rehearsals needed to happen. Plus, with that press release, there was the implication that Coachella would be a sort of trial balloon.

In any case, the tour quickly became massive in scope, while starting tiny, with a warm-up show at the Troubadour, April 1, 2016, in front of 500 lucky fans. A clutch of dates took place

throughout the rest of April with the next leg beginning in Detroit on June 23 and ending on August 22 in San Diego. In general, the band was playing stadiums to crowds of around forty thousand, virtually all sellouts. Next came South and Central America to close out the year, with Japan, New Zealand, and Australia getting a look at the new configuration in January and February of 2017. Next was an intensive European campaign, followed by a return to the United States, eating up May through September of 2017, again, mostly stadiums and again almost entirely sellouts. It was back to South America in late September and then North America once again to finish out the year, now downgraded to sports arenas. The never-ending tour picked up again in June 2018 in Europe, where the band consistently enjoyed their biggest crowds, routinely over forty thousand, and then into Asia and back to North America for a final cleanup at hockey barns. All told, the band grossed about $584 million across more than 150 shows, with venues filled to 96.8 percent capacity.

Support on the campaign was mostly local, with the more illustrious of the support acts including Lenny Kravitz, the Cult, Alice in Chains, Deftones, Live, Our Lady Peace, Babymetal, Wolfmother, the Darkness, Volbeat, and ZZ Top. Notable guest performers included Sebastian Bach, Pink, Dave Grohl, Billy Gibbons, Angus Young, Steven Adler, and, in Australia, Rose Tattoo's Angry Anderson, to perform "Nice Boys," of course.

As for interesting wrinkles in the tour, at a show in Germany in 2018, the band performed the Velvet Revolver hit "Slither." Early Guns N' Roses obscurity "Shadow of Your Love" also was played, with a few extra *Use Your Illusion* songs brought back and many *Chinese Democracy* songs remaining as regulars, now with Slash and Duff putting their personal stamp on them. Duff would step to the mic and play the punk rocker, sometimes taking the lead on the Damned's "New Rose," sometimes doing Iggy and the Stooges classic "Raw Power" instead.

Across the years, the band also had to deal with the deaths of Chris Cornell, playing "Black Hole Sun" for him, and Prince, with Duff festooning his bass with the initialized Prince symbol in tribute during the Coachella stand way at the beginning of this historic live run. Most surprising of all, in Edmonton, Alberta, August 30, 2017, celebrating the life of Glen Campbell who had just passed due to Alzheimer's disease, the band performed a version of "Wichita Lineman," proving that anything can happen at a GN'R show. It wouldn't be the last time for this one, and "Black Hole Sun" would be played again as well.

Left to right: Frank Ferrer, Richard Fortus, Dizzy Reed, Duff McKagan, Axl Rose, Slash, and Melissa Reese at Soldier Field, Chicago, July 3, 2016

So Alone

THE SOLO PROJECTS

Despite reflexive griping about Guns N' Roses not putting out enough records, when you add up the minutes, even under the banner brand name, there is a nice pile of music. But cast the net wider, ignoring or downplaying the name on the tin, it becomes sensible to include in the discography another half dozen albums, each one of them somewhat on the same level of legitimacy as *Chinese Democracy*. Cast the net wider, and one finds even more records that feel like they are part of the family stylistically, especially given the bold range Axl established for the band and brand with the aforementioned masterful platter-ful.

Duff begins the parade, with 1993's *Believe in Me*, followed by Slash in 1995 with *It's Five O'Clock Somewhere*, credited to Slash's Snakepit. Each of these albums reflected the personality of the respective Guns member, pertinently as close to that of the guy who was there on *Appetite for Destruction* and the *Use Your Illusion* duo. What's more, Duff's album included guest slots from Slash, Matt, Gilby, and Dizzy, along with Teddy Andreadis and West Arkeen. Slash's album was produced by Mike Clink and his five-piece band included Gilby and Matt, with Dizzy and Teddy guesting. Both of those albums had front covers that would have looked great slapped onto a GN'R album. Duff would be back soon as part of a supergroup called Neurotic Outsiders, for a one-and-done self-titled album in 1995.

"The original Snakepit lineup was a fluke," Slash explained back in 2000. "It was just killing time. I was still in Guns N' Roses at that point, and I was just trying to find something to do that was fun. I ended up making a record and doing a tour. Guns wasn't happening and I ended up leaving, so we put together what I would consider a permanent band to do Snakepit. It's just the different individuals that go to make up the band; it's all based on that. My style is always the same. We've all played with a whole bunch of different musicians, so this happens to be the particular Snakepit sound that everybody has invested in, with their time and talent and so on."

And although Izzy is no longer in the band, at the time, we all considered the self-titled Izzy Stradlin and the Ju-Ju Hounds album from 1992 as part of the family. Izzy quietly continued through the years, prolifically making solo albums, each more indie than the last, but telling us all we need to know about his personality and musical tastes and what he brought to Guns.

Similarly, Gilby Clarke would establish a solo path, with the two guitarists becoming the singer-songwriters of the extended family. As Gilby explained to me pertaining to his 1994 debut, "*Pawn Shop Guitars* was a collection of songs that I had already written, and in the end, when Guns was finished with the tour, I presented the songs to them, and they weren't really Guns N' Roses songs. So I said, well, let's just make my own record. It will give me something to do for the next year or so. So, it was songs I had from over the last few years, from '89 to '93. To me, the record has three different styles. It has some rock songs, some

I appreciate. And then when I went and made the second record, I took all of those three styles I liked and combined them in every song. I try to make records that are the kind of records that I would want to buy."

Slash's Snakepit returned in 2000 with a second and last album called *Ain't Life Grand*, and although the lineup is greatly diminished in terms of connections to the mothership, across the record's dozen fired-up songs, it's closer to traditional Guns than *Chinese Democracy*.

Explained Slash, with respect to the producer on the project, Jack Douglas, "Funnily enough, when Guns first got a record deal, Jack Douglas was my first choice as producer. But under the circumstances, there was a little too much chemical dependency going on between us and him, so the record company opted not to do that. Basically, like everything else with this whole fucking band, it came around full circle. He's clean and I'm clean, so he came down to a gig in Miami, which is probably one of the most

chaos going back and forth, but he said he would do it; that's how we got hooked up. But I would have loved to have had him way back in the day, if the situation had been a little bit different.

"When Jack came in, he was the glue," continues Slash. "We could relate to him. He was the only person who understood what the fucking band was all about. He was the only guy we met that wanted to make the same record we wanted to make. We're really just a bare-bones rock 'n' roll band with a bunch of clear-cut personalities. We're all good players, within reason. We are rock 'n' roll guys, so we're not that good. The spirit's there and the integrity is definitely fucking true."

Duff responded in 2001 with his *Dark Days* album under the band name Loaded, and has since done two more, as well as two more solo albums, on top of a shelved solo album in 1999 called *Beautiful Disease*. As Duff explained to me about Loaded, "In anything I've done, with Guns or with Velvet, I mean, you've definitely seeing my mark. So, my stamp is on Loaded too, as

Slash, Duff, Scott, Dave, and Matt of Velvet Revolver good for a first album in 2004 and a last one in 2007

much as it is on either of those two bands. But we definitely have our own twist. I don't know what kind of band we are. Sometimes we're like the heaviest death metal band, and sometimes we're a jangly, pop, nerdy Seattle band. But we're definitely a hard rock band. And we're honest. When we play live, I think that's what sets us apart. And the songwriting is honest too. It's not just Duff trying to line his pockets. We're a working rock band."

But it is the aforementioned Velvet Revolver that became the most notable of the extracurricular projects. The band featured Slash and Duff, along with Matt Sorum, Dave Kushner, and Scott Weiland from Stone Temple Pilots. Their first record, *Contraband*, from 2004, fell just shy of triple platinum in the United States, on the strength of smash singles "Slither" and "Fall to Pieces." A second and last, 2007's *Libertad*, failed to certify, but nonetheless, one could argue that given the personnel and the earthy, gunslinging sound of the band (even with Scott!) they are "of a set" with *Believe in Me, It's Five O'Clock Somewhere,* and *Chinese Democracy.*

"Usually everything is done in a day," chuckled Slash, speaking with the author about *Contraband*. "That's just the way the band works. There's only one spot, now that I think about it, where I actually went in and re-cut one song. I think a lot of it had to do with the fact that once we were done with the record, we were bored and sitting around. But one of the songs on the record didn't have the exact feel that we hoped it would have, and we went back and recorded it. So that was probably the only time we put in any sort of extra effort toward getting something right [*laughs*]. Everything else was pretty much written in a day and then recorded in a day. So it's all very natural for us. I mean, there's a lot of playing on there that can be challenging in places, but we just worked quickly, and you get over those hurdles pretty easily."

Slash says that there was one song influenced by Duff's and Dave's admiration for the Used, but for his own part, "The only song that had any influence coming from anywhere was 'Sucker Train Blues,' which represents what I like, bands like AC/DC and Aerosmith, even Cheap Trick and Van Halen, that kind of riffing. So, when I finally got the band on it [*laughs*], I was just happy that that song made the record because it represented a certain kind of style that had to do—more or less—with my hard-driven rock 'n' roll roots. The rest of it, to me, is just coming up with whatever you can. I never like to sit down and do something in homage to somebody else."

Izzy Stradlin and the Ju Ju Hounds, circa 1992. Left to right: Izzy Stradlin, Jimmy Ashurst, Rick Richards, and Charlie Quintana.

Gilby Clarke in Tokyo,
January 1992

SLASH
FEATURING MYLES KENNEDY
AND THE CONSPIRATORS

Wrapping things up, Slash also issued two albums under his own name. *Slash*, from 2010, features a bunch of songs he wrote the music for, topped with lyrics and vocals from various illustrious front men. *Orgy of the Damned*, from 2024, features both star singers as well as other star guitarists, doing mostly blues covers. But he also ventured back into the snakepit, as it were, with a band called Slash Featuring Myles Kennedy & the Conspirators, who were good for *Apocaplytic Love* in 2012, *World on Fire* in 2014, *Living the Dream* in 2018, and *4* in 2022. Slash's long history of collaboration with Kennedy made the superstar guitarist a regular visitor to all manner of venue big and small for years—Slash was not slacking.

The bottom line with all this is that Duff and Slash, with what they've done with their lives, have proven that they are in the rock 'n' roll game for the right reasons, and that should confirm one's confidence in what they've done as part of Guns. Slash wants to play guitar, on any size stage, and Duff is a punk rocker, writing and rocking roughshod, name on the tin be damned, have bass will travel, "Yes, I'll play on your record."

Matt is everywhere as well, and he's not done anything cooler than teaming up with Billy Gibbons, as the video to "West Coast Junkie" would attest. As we've mentioned, Izzy has exhibited a similar amount of sincerity and integrity, maybe even more, in his icy inclination to shun the spotlight and write intimate song after song. Last is Axl, who, both amusingly and enigmatically, has never done a side project, instead pouring a lifetime of loving

music into *Chinese Democracy*. Again, the message that falls out of this is that each of the core Gunners, during a life dedicated to rock 'n' roll, has quietly proven that they are for real, which is unquestionably one of the magic marker pointers as to why Guns N' Roses became one of the biggest and most beloved bands in the world.

"What's the motivation now?" reflected Duff, over the course of an interview we did about Loaded. "Man, I just think every band, you're kind of in search of that perfect album, or perfect song, at least. You're still chasing it. It doesn't matter. People will ask me, 'How come you're still chasing the perfect song?' I think any musician, it doesn't matter how old you are, how long you've been doing it, you're still chasing it and thinking, like, I haven't written *the* song. And we're a good band and we like each other and we genuinely love playing, creating music and touring together. And so those three things combined, you know, there is still a carrot out there. We're still pursuing what's out there somewhere."

Slash featuring Myles Kennedy and the Conspirators have managed an impressive run of four albums, with the lion's share of the songs being co-writes between Slash and Myles.

35
THIS I LOVE
Axl is in AC/DC!

If there were any vestiges left of Axl Rose's reputation needing continued rehabilitation, his run of twenty-three dates fronting AC/DC took care of the final strokes. The Aussie legends were struggling through the final dates promoting their anemic *Rock or Bust* album from 2014, when vocalist Brian Johnson had to give up the ghost, seemingly for good, due to his hearing being shot, although let's face it, screaming his head off for AC/DC since 1980 didn't help what was coming out either.

But the show must go on, so the band pulled the most attention-grabbing stunt possible and called upon the world's most famous singer—one from a single generation back, pointedly—to deputize for the beloved Newcastle fireplug. Also, credit to the amount of goodwill Axl had slowly clawed back by this point, AC/DC management had found probably the one guy on the planet that would quell any amount of refund-demanding fan revolt. This wasn't a compromise; rather, this was intensely surreal and disorienting history in the making. As for the grumblers, this was almost too garish a choice, with Axl's fame (and notoriety) turning the band more into a supergroup, not to mention the fact that Axl was both American and, relative to Angus, some kid who should be in a schoolboy uniform.

To make the flashy tale even more surreal, things got off to a shaky start when Axl busted his foot slipping onstage while shimmying N' shaking his way through "Mr. Brownstone" at a GN'R reunion tour warm-up show at the Troubadour, on April Fools' Day. Now he had to start his run with "Axl/DC" singing from a throne of sorts, following a similar situation Dave Grohl had gone through (Axl would, in fact, borrow Dave's throne), and somewhat presaging the effects of aging on our heroes, when Phil Collins would have to sing for Genesis from an old man chair. And it wasn't the first time Axl had done this either. Same thing happened at the last of three warm-up club shows at the Ritz in New York, just before the band was to hit the road living large and promoting the *Use the Illusion* albums. On that occasion, the cursed song was "You Could Be Mine," with Axl taking an acrobatic jump and landing badly. He didn't sit for subsequent shows, but he had to wear a leg brace.

Axl/DC on the *Rock or Bust* tour, Auburn Hills, Michigan, September 9, 2016

Back in black or a touch too much? Axl with AC/DC, Etihad Stadium, Manchester, United Kingdom, June 9, 2016. Looking on, Angus and Stevie Young.

That first show with AC/DC took place in Lisbon, Portugal, May 7, 2016, and he was equally hobbled for his temp job in Seville, Marseilles, Paris, and a festival date in Wechter, Belgium. Vienna was slated for May 19, and by then Axl was back on his feet. Brian Johnson didn't sound like Bon Scott and Axl sounded like neither of them, but somehow at the howling end of Axl's range, which was called for often, it all made sense. AC/DC played a total of thirteen shows in Europe with Axl and then took a summer break. Yet Axl didn't get downtime; he transitioned right into tour dates with the Gunners. Ten shows took place in America, August 27 through September 20, with Axl signing off in Philadelphia after a total of twenty-three shows in the books.

As for the set list with AC/DC, as the tour progressed, Axl influenced its contours, including a slight expansion. In fact, the first change took place right way, with the band adding "Riff Raff" and "Rock 'n' Roll Damnation," both from 1978's *Powerage*, a top-ranked album by many AC/DC scholars (Axl would have been sixteen at the time, and fully in the throes of it). But even those two songs are popular and somewhat unsurprising compared to *Highway to Hell* deep tracks "If You Want Blood (You've Got It)," which was added to the set a week later, and the even deeper (and heaver) "Touch Too Much," which was played on three occasions. Performed on one occasion was "Dog Eat Dog" and also added to the set as a regular was "Live Wire." The sum total of all that is that the set got longer, and every added selection was from the Bon Scott era, which was more suited to Axl's voice and, let's face it, his preference as a headbanger born and bred in the '70s.

For his part, Brian went on record as somewhat traumatized by Axl taking his gig, with Brian finding the experience difficult to watch and stating in his autobiography that he's never seen footage of it. Slash, on the other hand, turned out to be both impressed and proud of Axl, also pointing out how hard Axl worked to make sure he made the best of the opportunity. At the end of the tour, Axl thanked Grohl for the use of his throne by gifting him an early-'60s Gibson ES-335 Dot guitar, personally selected by Slash.

As it turned out, Brian would embark on a journey of rehabilitation with some cutting-edge aural technology and he'd be back for at least light duty, not to mention a whole new studio album in 2020 called *Power Up*—far as I remember, there was no new studio album from Guns N' Roses in 2020.

Can I sit next to you, girl?
Ernst Happel Stadion,
Vienna, May 19, 2016.

36
USED TO LOVE HER

Appetite for Destruction subject
of elaborate reissue

Who put the "B" in box? That would be Geffen and Axl and his imagining mind, because *Appetite for Destruction: Locked N' Loaded* is pretty much the most insane and excessive box set ever done, at least for a single album. The campaign started early, with billboards going up on April 30, 2018, announcing "Destruction is coming" and a corresponding countdown campaign on the band's website. Next, on May 21, came the release of the vintage 1989 video for "It's So Easy," rarely used back in the day and previously not officially released, followed by promotional videos for some of the more interesting artifacts.

Then, on June 29, 2018, came the release of the box, as well as the cut-back Deluxe Edition and Super Deluxe Edition, with much hoopla taking place at record and CD stores around the world. As alluded to, the monster package set a new high watermark for design. The contents were packaged in a big wooden box with the GN'R cross logo from the debut rendered in 3D on the front and carved-look images around it etched into the black box. The doors swing open like a closet wardrobe, left and right, revealing slots plus six adorable little drawers. Inside were reproduction handbills and ticket stubs, a numbered certificate of authenticity, buttons, stickers, temporary tattoos, patches, photos, posters, a turntable mat, a record-cleaning cloth, a hologram, a bandana, a concert banner, metal picks, skull rings, skull pins, and a commemorative 2-inch (5 cm) coin, along with twelve lithograph illustrations, each inspired by one of the dozen songs on the debut. The paper goods were thoughtfully

Opposite: An old-school record company billboard looms over the Sunset Strip in Hollywood, promoting the *Appetite for Destruction* deluxe reissue program.

Below: Guns N' Roses in 1987. Who knew?

The sweet and innocent crafters of *Appetite for Destruction*, 1987

housed in red, black, and yellow blind-embossed cardboard envelopes matching the design of the hardshell box itself. Also included was a ninety-six-page hardcover booklet stuffed with live photography and shots of flyers, passes, press materials, ads, 7-inch singles, and other collected artifacts from Axl's personal archive. Finally, because it could not be ignored, there was a litho print of the controversial original cover art for the album by Robert Williams, one side depicting the aftermath of a rape scene, the other depicting the pouncing machine monster that ostensibly is going to make things right.

As for the music, the *Locked N' Loaded* version sensibly contains the biggest trawl, available on CD, vinyl, and a 32GB cross logo USB featuring three different resolution levels. There was also a cassette tape of 1985 Mystic Studio Session demos hidden in one of the drawers, plus some 45 rpm records, complete with an adaptor for your turntable spindle. In total, the box contains four CDs, one Blu-ray, seven LPs, and seven 45s on yellow vinyl.

The first CD contains the package anchor, namely a remastered version of the original *Appetite for Destruction* album. The second CD is called *B-Sides N' Eps* and is essentially a revisitation of the debut EP plus assorted live things. The third disc is called *1986 Sound City Sessions*, commemorating the recording the band did with Manny Charlton, which continues on disc four, *1986 Sound City Sessions N' More*. The Blu-ray contains 5.1 surround sound and remastered stereo versions of the album and additional bits and pieces, including video.

The Super Deluxe Edition includes the same music as found on *Locked N' Loaded*, while the smallest packed, the Deluxe Edition, is the original album on one CD and a second seventy-three-minute CD containing eighteen of the rarities.

All told, we get to hear all manner of demo and live versions of songs that made the debut (and how already considered, structured, and mapped out they were quite early on), but we also get an appreciation for just how much material, looking back and forward, was available to appear on the debut, especially if one considers covers. The non-*Appetite* originals on offer consist of "Reckless Life," "Move to the City," "Shadow of Your Love," "Patience," "Used to Love Her," "Ain't Goin' Down No More," "The Plague," "Back Off Bitch," "New Work Tune," "November Rain," and "Don't Cry." As for covers, we get to hear "Nice Boys," "Mama Kin," "Knockin' on Heaven's Door," "Whole Lotta Rosie," "Heartbreak Hotel," and "Jumpin' Jack Flash." Granted it's not a lot of significantly new music, with the highlights being Zeppelin-esque acoustic jam "New Work Tune," the brief but complete "The Plague," and most substantially, full rocker "Ain't Goin' Down No More."

The *Locked N' Loaded* box was originally produced in an edition of ten thousand and sold for $1,000. It soon went down to half that, at one point selling officially for $399. It's now firmly become a collectible and is up over $1,000 again, and sure to keep rising. Various components of it were being sold separately right from the band's own merchandise site, offering many ways to get these goodies, but now those bits and pieces are no longer there, nor is the complete box. In any event, the end result of this campaign is that *Appetite for Destruction* reentered the top ten of the *Billboard* charts and more saliently, Guns N' Roses continues to be one of the biggest bands in the world in terms of live receipts, still significantly because of the debut that would not die and now underscored by this elegant new celebration of *Appetite for Destruction*'s eternal grip on the rock 'n' roll masses. Still, Guns N' Roses were not all-powerful: even though *Locked N' Loaded* was nominated for a box set design Grammy, it lost out to a Weird Al Yankovic box housed in a replica accordion.

37
DUST N' BONES

Band embarks on We're F'N' Back! tour

Pink performs with the
band on day two of the 2021
BottleRock Napa Valley
Festival, Napa, California,
September 4, 2021.

Guns N' Roses were hit by COVID just like everybody, having to cancel a July 2020 tour, with Smashing Pumpkins supporting, after just one date, on March 14 in Mexico City. It was a festival date and other bands had pulled out, but almost foreshadowing what was to come, Axl and the boys stood fast and put in a twenty-two-song performance, including the first airing of "So Fine" since 1993. A European and North America tour also was canceled, as the pandemic took hold in the spring of 2020 and the search was on for a vaccine and other procedures to mitigate the bug.

But on July 21, 2021, in Hershey, Pennsylvania, the band began execution of the We're F'N' Back! tour, rolling on generally unscathed through a US campaign ending on October 2 and 3 at the Hard Rock Live in Hollywood, Florida, in front of twelve thousand fans each night. Supporting throughout was Mammoth WVH, poetically, given that each band in its own way is a chip off the Van Halen block. The venues picked were a mix of indoor and outdoor locales with scaled-down crowds in the low- to mid-five figures. Wolfgang's band had to cancel a couple of shows due to COVID, but the Gunners managed to get through unbugged, although Axl contracted a case of food poisoning halfway through in Chicago—he soldiered on at Wrigley Field, nonetheless.

With respect to avoiding COVID, as Slash explained it, the guys were just super careful, limiting interactions with fans or folks on the industry before or after the shows and just playing live and getting out of Dodge. As for the band members, it was straight from the hotel to the stage and then back to the hotel, with the most notable change in procedure being the lack of extravagant after-parties, a GN'R trademark. Slash stayed sane by taking on outside projects that he could work on from his hotel room, and for his part, Richard Fortus said he stayed healthy through almost habitual jogging and going to the gym.

Both Slash and Myles Kennedy wound up getting COVID while working on their *4* album, but, somewhat ironically, Guns N' Roses was one of the most responsible organizations navigating the often-ridiculous waters of the concert industry during the pandemic. While others fell ill and postponed, the Gunners managed to play all twenty-five of their shows and every time with a full slate of band members. Taking a positive view, Slash found appeal in the reduction of craziness on the road, and he also gained a new appreciation for how cool a job he had.

Bottom line: The band was back to playing in stadiums to crowds averaging fifty thousand for a European tour leg running from June 4 through July 15, 2022. Support came from Gary Clark Jr. and the band was joined onstage by Carrie Underwood on two occasions, helping sing "Sweet Child o' Mine" and "Paradise City." This was followed by an intensive South American campaign, ending with four October dates in Mexico. To wrap up the year, the band played to brand as world citizens of the rock community, visiting Japan, Thailand, Singapore, Australia, and New Zealand. Final score: Guns N' Roses, 1; COVID, nil.

38
BAD APPLES
GN'R issues "Absurd" and "Hard Skool"

A dozen years on since *Chinese Democracy*, Guns N' Roses emerges with a new song, just in time for a new spate of dates. "Absurd," issued as a single on August 6, 2021, is a Guns-ified reworking of a *Chinese Democracy* sessions song called "Silkworms," written by keyboardists Chris Pitman and Dizzy Reed. Played live four times back in 2001, "Silkworms" is more radical, atonal, atmospheric, and industrial compared to "Absurd," but retained faithfully is Axl's bratty monotone vocal, sent extra extreme with a bullhorn effect.

Credited to Axl, Dizzy, Slash, and Duff, "Absurd" features emboldened guitar chords, but like "Silkworms," it is still a frantic, claustrophobic, and experimental song, to the point where it's the strangest and most future-forward thing Slash and Duff have ever been associated with, sort of in a Tool, Janes Addiction,

or even Voivod zone. Predictably, reviews were mixed, but had Axl put a less angry and noisy vocal on it, the song might have fared better. As it stands, it's admirably creative, relentlessly heavy, and yes, even at the guitar end, obscure in the spirit of the early 2000s band and defiantly anti-commercial. Drumming on the song is Brain, and helping Axl produce the track is Axl's weirdness-enabler Caram Costanzo, who also co-produced *Chinese Democracy*.

Two months later, September 24, came another new song, "Hard Skool." Beginning life as "Checkmate," then "Jackie Chan," and then "Hard School," the song is closer to traditional Guns N' Roses compared to "Absurd," representing a cogent alloy between Slash's gunslinging guitar playing and Duff's punk-rocking and sharpened bass sound. But again, it's got a weird vocal, with Axl singing clean inside of a sing-songy vocal melody. Once again Brain drums and Caram Costanzo co-produces, although sonically, "Hard Skool" could have slotted right in on the Use Your Illusion albums, in large part due to the carnal tone Slash and Mike Clink managed to locate back in 1991, even if the spark was already present back at *Appetite*.

"Absurd" and "Hard Skool" were combined into a CD EP and cassette for issue on January 28, 2022. Also included were live versions of "Don't Cry" and "You're Crazy." Two versions on 7-inch vinyl were produced. The first combined "Hard Skool" with a live version of "Absurd." The second, on clear vinyl and issued to the Nightrain fan club in June 2022, added a live version of "Shadow of Your Love."

Together, the new tracks represented logically the "Velvet Roses" version of the modern-day GN'R, a synthesis of Axl's radicalism and the traditional, anchoring Aerosmith rock presence of Slash and Duff. In fact, "Absurd" on its own performs that feat, offering some of the most heroic guitar chords of the ragged catalog. "Hard Skool" is more curious. Given its roots also in the *Chinese Democracy* era of the band, it perhaps points to the fact that Axl is more old-school GN'R than the story would suggest, which, one supposes, is why he's broken bread with Slash and Duff for more years recently than he ever did back in the glory days.

This page and opposite: GN'R at the Banc of California Stadium, Los Angeles, August 19, 2021.

39
YESTERDAYS
Geffen issues *Use Your Illusion* expanded editions

On November 11, 2022, Geffen reprised the glory they created with the *Appetite for Destruction* reissue program and rolled out new versions of the *Use Your Illusion* records, each in a Deluxe Edition and combined as the mammoth Super Deluxe Edition.

Included in the full box package was a one-hundred-page hardcover booklet, a replica fan club folder and membership card, replica fan club newsletters, ten lithograph illustrations that offer different pictures when filtered through red and blue mylar "reveal" sleeves, 8" x 10" photos of the band, a poster, some replica concert passes, and a replica ticket. There was a twelve-LP (plus one Blu-ray) version and a seven-CD (also with the same Blu-ray) version, with the Deluxe Edition configuration being two CDs, which contain some live material that isn't part of the Super Deluxe Edition. These

also include twenty-four-page booklets. The albums were also reissued as two LP sets, a four-LP vinyl box, plus remastered single CDs, resulting in nine separate pieces of product at once.

With respect to the extra music, unfortunately it's all GN'R live in concert, outside of a new version of "November Rain" with orchestra. But it's two full concerts: Live in New York, from the Ritz Theatre, May 16, 1991, and Live in Las Vegas, from the Thomas & Mach Center, January 25, 1992. The Live in New York show features Shannon Hoon as guest on two tracks, "Don't Cry" and "You Ain't the First." The Blind Melon frontman was a friend of the band who died in 1995 of a cocaine overdose at the age of twenty-eight. A favorite extra from the Las Vegas show is the brief bit of Pink Floyd's "Mother" before the "Paradise City" encore. The Bu-ray in both the CD and LP packages provides an audiovisual rendition of the New York show.

As alluded to, the two CD editions, instead of the complete New York or Las Vegas concerts, offer up compilations from many shows. Highlights on the bonus disc from *Use Your Illusion I* include the band with Lenny Kravitz on his hit song "Always on the Run" along with "Attitude" from *"The Spaghetti Incident?"* plus covers of Black Sabbath's "It's Alright" and the Stones' "Wild Horses," all recorded in Paris. The *Use Your Illusion II* bonus disc features a number of cover-related oddities, including Axl's uneasy a cappella snippet of Queen's "Sail Away Sweet Sister," the instrumental "Only Women Bleed" intro to "Knockin' on Heaven's Door," plus "Mama Kin" and "Train Kept a-Rollin'," both with Joe Perry and Steven Tyler guesting. There's also the band's famed power ballad arrangement of "Speak Softly, Love (Love Theme from *The Godfather*)," which I always thought added a touch of class to any given Guns N' Roses show.

This page and opposite: Guns N' Roses were in the throes of promoting their long-awaited *Use Your Illusion* albums when they turned in a stunning performance at the April 20, 1992, *Freddie Mercury Tribute Concert* in London.

40
DOUBLE TALKIN' JIVE
New single renews hope for new album

As our story draws to a close, we're left with more questions than answers. News from the Guns N' Roses camp has been quiet, with both Slash and Duff going back to making music on their own. And yet, intriguingly, there's been another couple of new songs, making that four since 2021. First came "Perhaps," a tough, strident, full-band ballad with Axl reflective inside of the lyrics and singing passionately over pumping piano. The song was issued as a digital single on August 18, 2023, with a 7-inch version arriving in December of that year.

On the backside of the single was a new song called "The General," which found the GN'R collective in the same psychological backrooms as "Absurd" as well as points along the *Chinese Democracy* album that evoke a similar state of agitation and paranoia. In fact, upholding the band's incendiary punk rock and shock rock ethic, "The General" might be the most divisive Guns N' Roses song of all time, given its atonal, psychedelic spooky-core lope and electronically treated Axl vocal.

You listen to these two songs—one very commercial and accessible and the other obstinately the opposite—and what does this tell us about where Axl and his two-headed beast of a backing band is going to go, if and when we get a follow-up to *Chinese Democracy*? Fact is, the beauty of the situation is that we are completely on tenterhooks—intrigued, baffled, and excited.

But we're also comfortable and confirmed with our realization that even if *Appetite for Destruction* from way back in 1987 was—let's face it—pretty much just a really good version of standard lunch bucket rock 'n' roll, the band has grown into a collective of great artists. It's Slash and Duff and Dizzy as enthusiastic and encyclopedic translators and transmitters of timeless rock 'n' roll. It's also Richard, Frank, and Melissa as new blood and new ideas and new technologies, with Bumblefoot, Buckethead, and Brain inflicting the most psychic damage on Axl Rose along the way, only making him a better musician. But in the end, it's Axl as flashpoint and fulcrum, as the synthesis and the best version of all the above, leading the charge, proven by the four new songs to be fearless about—and impervious to—any admonitions that might come his way.

In other words, if we ever see that follow-up to *Chinese Democracy*, we know it's going to be soaked in the spirit of hard-birthed art-making. And who knows if the lineup will even be the same, although we suspect it's still going to be the work of a meeting of many minds, again, each providing a puzzle piece or two to the exasperating full picture Axl has rattling around his head. Until then, like it's always been, there's the muscle memory of staying toned and in tune by playing live. Fortunately for Guns N' Roses, millions of people around the world are happy to help keep the band in fighting trim, patient for whenever Axl might resume his creative odyssey.

Guns N' Roses headline the Pyramid stage as the sun sets on the Glastonbury Festival, Worthy Farm, Glastonbury, June 24, 2023.

DISCOGRAPHY

Concerning a few points on format, I've included an additional notes section for anything I thought was interesting, that seemed important. I've left the double quote marks off the song titles here to keep things tidy, although you will see them in the notes section, given that the format there is prosy. I've noted side 1/side 2 designations for all releases from the vinyl era, which I've always maintained ends in 1990. For Guns N' Roses, that would mean *GN'R Lies* is our last chunk of vinyl. Credits on *Live Era '87–'93* and *Greatest Hits* are pared back a bit, again, for tidiness.

Now, obviously, this is a messy catalog, but also, mercifully, not extensive. As a result of both those points, I've decided to present this in something of a novel manner. First, I'm only citing releases I've deemed significant, which rules out reissues and anything shorter than an EP (*Hard Skool* is more of an extended single). Second, everything is presented chronologically, mixing together the various release types, where usually, certainly with a bigger catalog, I'd compartmentalize into studio, live, and compilation categories. The idea here is to mirror the story as expressed in the body of the book.

LIVE ?!*@ LIKE A SUICIDE

December 16, 1986

UZI Suicide USR-001

Produced by Guns N' Roses

Side 1: 1. Reckless Life (Rose, Slash, Stradlin, Weber) 3:23; 2. Nice Boys (Wells, Anderson, Ryall, Leach, Cocks) 3:01; 3. Move to the City (Stradlin, D.J., Weber) 3:41; 4. Mama Kin (Tyler) 3:57

Notes: four-track EP. The same tracks are repeated on side 2. "Nice Boys" is a Rose Tattoo cover and "Mama Kin" is an Aerosmith cover. The band's initial lineup consists of W. Axl Rose—vocals, Slash—guitars, Izzy Stradlin—guitars, Duff "Rose" McKagan—bass, Steven Adler—drums.

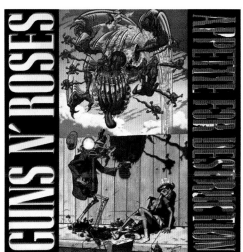

APPETITE FOR DESTRUCTION

July 21, 1987

Geffen GHS 24148

Produced by Mike Clink

Side 1: Welcome to the Jungle 4:31; 2. It's So Easy (Guns N' Roses, Arkeen) 3:21; 3. Nightrain 4:26; 4. Out ta Get Me 4:20; 5. Mr. Brownstone 3:46; 6. Paradise City 6:46

Side 2: My Michelle 3:39; 2. Think About You 3:50; 3. Sweet Child o' Mine 5:55; 4. You're Crazy 3:25; 5. Anything Goes (Guns N' Roses, Weber) 3:25; 6. Rocket Queen

Notes: debut studio album. All songs written by Guns N' Roses unless otherwise stated. Same lineup as debut EP.

GN'R LIES

November 29, 1988

Geffen GHS 24198

Produced by Guns N' Roses (side one) and Mike Clink (side two)

Side 1: 1. Reckless Life (Rose, Slash, Stradlin, Weber) 3:20; 2. Nice Boys (Wells, Anderson, Ryall, Leach, Cocks) 3:02; 3. Move to the City (Stradlin, D.J., Weber) 3:42; 4. Mama Kin (Tyler) 3:54

Side 2: 1. Patience (Guns N' Roses) 5:53; 2. Used to Love Her (Guns N' Roses) 3:10; 3. You're Crazy (Guns N' Roses) 4:08; 4. One in a Million (Guns N' Roses) 6:08

Notes: This album consists of the band's *Live ?!*@ Like a Suicide* EP along with four new originals recorded acoustically.

USE YOUR ILLUSION I

September 17, 1991

Geffen GEFD-24415

Produced by Mike Clink and Guns N' Roses

1. Right Next Door to Hell (Rose, Stradlin, Kaltio) 2:58; 2. Dust N' Bones (McKagan, Stradlin, Slash) 4:55; 3. Live and Let Die (Paul McCartney, Linda McCartney) 2:59; 4. Don't Cry (Original) (Rose, Stradlin) 4:42; 5. Perfect Crime (Rose, Stradlin, Slash) 2:22; 6. You Ain't the First (Stradlin) 2:32; 7. Bad Obsession (Stradlin, Arkeen) 5:26; 8. Back Off Bitch (Rose, Tobias) 5:01; 9. Double Talkin' Jive (Stradlin) 3:19; 10. November Rain (Rose) 8:53; 11. The Garden (Rose, James, Arkeen) 5:17; 12. Garden of Eden (Rose, Slash) 2:36; 13. Don't Damn Me (Rose, Lank, Slash) 5:15; 14. Bad Apples (Rose, MacKagan, Stradlin, Slash) 4:25; 15. Dead Horse (Rose) 4:17; 16. Coma (Rose, Slash) 10:08

Notes: For the simultaneously released *Use Your Illusion I* and *Use Your Illusion II*, drummer Steven Adler is replaced by Matt Sorum and the band add a keyboardist, Dizzy Reed.

USE YOUR ILLUSION II

September 17, 1991

Geffen GEFD-24420

Produced by Mike Clink and Guns N' Roses

1. Civil War (Rose, McKagan, Slash) 7:36; 2. 14 Years (Rose, Stradlin) 4:17; 3. Yesterdays (Rose, Arkeen, James, McCloud) 3:13; 4. Knockin' on Heaven's Door (Dylan) 5:36; 5. Get in the Ring (Rose, McKagan, Slash) 5:29; 6. Shotgun Blues (Rose) 3:23; 7. Breakdown (Rose) 6:58; 8. Pretty Fucked Up (Stradlin) 4:46; 9. Locomotive (Rose, Slash) 8:42; 10. So Fine (McKagan) 4:09; 11. Estranged (Rose) 9:20; 12. You Could Be Mine (Rose, Stradlin) 5:48; 13. Don't Cry (Alt. Lyrics) (Rose, Stradlin) 4:42; 14. My World (Rose) 1:22

"THE SPAGHETTI INCIDENT?"

November 23, 1993

Geffen GEFD-24617

Produced by Mike Clink and Guns N' Roses, except "Since I Don't Have You" produced by Guns N' Roses and "You Can't Put Your Arms Around a Memory" produced by Duff McKagan and Jim Mitchell

1. Since I Don't Have You (Joseph Rock, James Beaumont and the Skyliners) 4:18; 2. New Rose (Brian James) 2:38; 3. Down on the Farm (Charles Harper, Alvin Gibbs, Nicholas Garrett) 3:23; 4. Human Being (Johnny Thunders, David Johansen) 4:32; 5. Raw Power (Iggy Pop, James Williamson) 3:10; 6. Ain't It Fun (Cheetah Chrome, Peter Laughner) 4:59; 7. Buick Makane (Big Dumb Sex) (Buick Makane by Marc Boan; Big Dumb Sex by Chrstopher J. Cornell) 2:37; 8. Hair of the Dog (Dan McCafferty, Pete Agnew, Manuel Charlton, Darrell Sweet) 3:57; 9. Attitude (Glenn Danzig) 1:29; 10. Black Leather (Steven Jones) 3:45; 11. You Can't Put Your Arms Around a Memory (Johnny Thunders) 3:34; 12. I Don't Care About You (Lee Ving) 2:03; 13. Look at Your Game Girl (Charles Manson) 2:34

Notes: Covers album. Final track is uncredited and plays as track 13, with track 12 being nine seconds of silence. Guitarist Izzy Stradlin is replaced by Gilby Clarke. Assorted guest performers in minor roles.

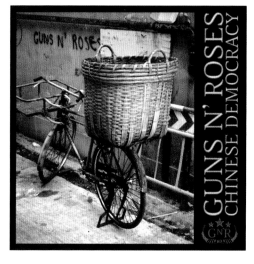

LIVE ERA '87-'93

November 23, 1999

Geffen 0694905142

Produced by Del James

CD1: 1. Nightrain 5:19; 2. Mr. Brownstone 5:42;
3. It's So Easy 3:28; 4. Welcome to the Jungle 5:09;
5. Dust N' Bones 5:05; 6. My Michelle 3:53; 7. You're
Crazy 4:45; 8. Used to Love Her 4:17; 9. Patience
6:42; 10. It's Alright (Bill Ward) 3:07; 11. November
Rain 12:32

CD2: 1. Out ta Get Me 4:33; 2. Pretty Tied Up 5:25;
3. Yesterdays 3:52; 4. Move to the City 8:00;
5. You Could Be Mine 6:02; 6. Rocket Queen 8:27;
7. Sweet Child o' Mine 7:25; 8. Knockin' on Heaven's
Door 7:27; 9. Don't Cry 4:44; 10. Estranged 9:52;
11. Paradise City 7:22

Notes: A compilation of live recordings from 1987,
1988, 1991, 1992, and 1993, thus featuring various
lineups.

GREATEST HITS

March 23, 2004

Geffen B0001714-02

1. Welcome to the Jungle 4:33; 2. Sweet Child o'
Mine 5:57; 3. Shadow of Your Love 3:06; 4. Patience
5:56; 5. Paradise City 6:46; 6. Knockin' on Heaven's
Door 5:36; 7. Civil War 7:40; 8. You Could Be Mine
5:44; 9. Don't Cry 4:44; 10. November Rain 8:57;
11. Live and Let Die 3:02; 12. Yesterdays 3:14;
13. Ain't It Fun 5:07; 14. Since I Don't Have You
4:19; 15. Sympathy for the Devil (Mick Jagger, Keith
Richards) 7:36

CHINESE DEMOCRACY

November 23, 2008

Geffen/Black Frog B0012356-02

Produced by Axl Rose and Caram Costanzo,
additional production by Roy Thomas Baker

1. Chinese Democracy (Rose, Freese, Tobias,
Stinson, Reed, Finck, Costanzo, Cadieux) 4:43;
2. Shackler's Revenge (Rose, Finck, Carroll,
Costanzo, Mantia, Scaturro) 3:37; 3. Better (Rose,
Finck) 4:58; 4. Street of Dreams (Rose, Finck, Reed,
Stinson, Tobias) 4:46; 5. If the World (Rose, Pitman)
4:54; 6. There Was a Time (Rose, Tobias, Reed,
Stinson) 6:41; 7. Catcher in the Rye (Rose, Stinson,
Reed, Finck, Tobias) 5:53; 8. Scraped (Rose, Carroll,
Costanzo) 3:30; 9. Riad N' the Bedouins (Rose,
Finck, Reed, Stinson, Tobias) 4:10; 10. Sorry (Rose,
Carroll, Mantia, Scaturro) 6:14; 11. I.R.S. (Rose,
Tobias, Reed) 4:28; 12. Madagascar (Rose, Pitman)
5:38; 13. This I Love (Rose) 5:34; 14. Prostitute (Rose,
Finck, Tobias) 6:15

Notes: A summary version of the lineup for this
album would include principal Axl Rose, along with
Robin Finck, Bumblefoot (Ron Thal), Buckethead
(Brian Carroll), Paul Tobias, and Richard Fortus
on guitars; Tommy Stinson on bass; Brain (Brian
Mantia) and Frank Ferrer on drums; and Dizzy Reed
and Chris Pitman on keyboards.

ABOUT THE AUTHOR

At approximately 7,900 (with over 7,000 appearing in his books), Martin has unofficially written more record reviews than anybody in the history of music writing across all genres. Additionally, Martin has penned approximately 130 books on hard rock, heavy metal, prog, punk, classic rock, and record collecting. He was editor-in-chief of the now retired *Brave Words & Bloody Knuckles*, Canada's foremost metal publication for fourteen years, and has also contributed to *Revolver, Guitar World, Goldmine, Record Collector*, bravewords.com, lollipop.com, and hardradio.com, with many record label band bios and liner notes to his credit as well. Additionally, Martin has been a regular contractor to Banger Films, having worked for two years as researcher on the award-winning documentary *Rush: Beyond the Lighted Stage*, on the writing and research team for the eleven-episode *Metal Evolution*, and on the ten-episode *Rock Icons*, both for VH1 Classic. Additionally, Martin is the writer of the original heavy metal genre chart used in *Metal: A Headbanger's Journey* and throughout the *Metal Evolution* episodes. He also has a weekly podcast called *History in Five Songs with Martin Popoff* and is part of a YouTube channel called *The Contrarians*. Martin currently resides in Toronto and can be reached through martinp@inforamp.net or www.martinpopoff.com.

AUTHOR BIBLIOGRAPHY

2024
Behind the Lines: Genesis on Record: 1978–1997, Entangled: Genesis on Record 1969–1976, Run with the Wolf: Rainbow on Record, Van Halen at 50, Honesty Is No Excuse: Thin Lizzy on Record, Pictures at Eleven: Robert Plant Album by Album, Perfect Water: The Rebel Imaginos

2023: *Kiss at 50, The Electric Church: The Biography, Dominance and Submission: The Blue Öyster Cult Canon, The Who and Quadrophenia, Wild Mood Swings: Disintegrating The Cure Album by Album, AC/DC at 50*

2022: *Pink Floyd and The Dark Side of the Moon: 50 Years; Killing the Dragon: Dio in the '90s and 2000s; Feed My Frankenstein: Alice Cooper, the Solo Years; Easy Action: The Original Alice Cooper Band; Lively Arts: The Damned Deconstructed; Yes: A Visual Biography II: 1982–2022; Bowie at 75; Dream Evil: Dio in the '80s; Judas Priest: A Visual Biography; UFO: A Visual Biography*

2021: *Hawkwind: A Visual Biography, Loud 'n' Proud: Fifty Years of Nazareth, Yes: A Visual Biography, Uriah Heep: A Visual Biography, Driven: Rush in the '90s and "In the End," Flaming Telepaths: Imaginos Expanded and Specified, Rebel Rouser: A Sweet User Manual*

2020: *The Fortune: On the Rocks with Angel, Van Halen: A Visual Biography, Limelight: Rush in the '80s, Thin Lizzy: A Visual Biography, Empire of the Clouds: Iron Maiden in the 2000s, Blue Öyster Cult: A Visual Biography, Anthem: Rush in the '70s, Denim and Leather: Saxon's First Ten Years, Black Funeral: Into the Coven with Mercyful Fate*

2019: *Satisfaction: 10 Albums That Changed My Life, Holy Smoke: Iron Maiden in the '90s, Sensitive to Light: The Rainbow Story, Where Eagles Dare: Iron Maiden in the '80s, Aces High: The Top 250 Heavy Metal Songs of the '80s, Judas Priest: Turbo 'til Now, Born Again! Black Sabbath in the Eighties and Nineties*

2018: *Riff Raff: The Top 250 Heavy Metal Songs of the '70s, Lettin' Go: UFO in the '80s and '90s, Queen: Album by Album, Unchained: A Van Halen User Manual, Iron Maiden: Album by Album, Sabotage! Black Sabbath in the Seventies, Welcome to My Nightmare: 50 Years of Alice Cooper, Judas Priest: Decade of Domination, Popoff Archive – 6: American Power Metal, Popoff Archive – 5: European Power Metal, The Clash: All the Albums, All the Songs*

2017: *Led Zeppelin: All the Albums, All the Songs, AC/DC: Album by Album, Lights Out: Surviving the '70s with UFO, Tornado of Souls: Thrash's Titanic Clash, Caught in a Mosh: The Golden Era of Thrash, Rush: Album by Album, Beer Drinkers and Hell Raisers: The Rise of Motörhead, Metal Collector: Gathered Tales from Headbangers, Hit the Lights: The Birth of Thrash, Popoff Archive – 4: Classic Rock, Popoff Archive – 3: Hair Metal*

2016: *Popoff Archive – 2: Progressive Rock, Popoff Archive – 1: Doom Metal, Rock the Nation: Montrose, Gamma and Ronnie Redefined, Punk Tees: The Punk Revolution in 125 T-Shirts, Metal Heart: Aiming High with Accept, Ramones at 40, Time and a Word: The Yes Story*

2015: *Kickstart My Heart: A Mötley Crüe Day-by-Day, This Means War: The Sunset Years of the NWOBHM, Wheels of Steel: The Explosive Early Years of the NWOBHM, Swords and Tequila: Riot's Classic First Decade, Who Invented Heavy Metal?, Sail Away: Whitesnake's Fantastic Voyage*

2014: *Live Magnetic Air: The Unlikely Saga of the Superlative Max Webster, Steal Away the Night: An Ozzy Osbourne Day-by-Day, The Big Book of Hair Metal, Sweating Bullets: The Deth and Rebirth of Megadeth, Smokin' Valves: A Headbanger's Guide to 900 NWOBHM Records*

2013: *The Art of Metal* (co-edit with Malcolm Dome), *2 Minutes to Midnight: An Iron Maiden Day-by-Day, Metallica: The Complete Illustrated History, Rush: The Illustrated History, Ye Olde Metal: 1979, Scorpions: Top of the Bill*--updated and reissued as *Wind of Change: The Scorpions Story* in 2016

2012: *Epic Ted Nugent, Fade To Black: Hard Rock Cover Art of the Vinyl Age, It's Getting Dangerous: Thin Lizzy 81–12, We Will Be Strong: Thin Lizzy 76–81, Fighting My Way Back: Thin Lizzy 69–76, The Deep Purple Royal Family: Chain of Events '80–'11, The Deep Purple Royal Family: Chain of Events Through '79* - reissued as *The Deep Purple Family Year by Year* books

2011: *Black Sabbath FAQ, The Collector's Guide to Heavy Metal: Volume 4: The '00s* (co-authored with David Perri)

2010: *Goldmine Standard Catalog of American Records 1948 – 1991, 7th Edition*

2009: *Goldmine Record Album Price Guide, 6th Edition, Goldmine 45 RPM Price Guide, 7th Edition, A Castle Full of Rascals: Deep Purple '83–'09, Worlds Away: Voivod and the Art of Michel Langevin, Ye Olde Metal: 1978*

2008: *Gettin' Tighter: Deep Purple '68–'76, All Access: The Art of the Backstage Pass, Ye Olde Metal: 1977, Ye Olde Metal: 1976*

2007: *Judas Priest: Heavy Metal Painkillers, Ye Olde Metal: 1973 to 1975, The Collector's Guide to Heavy Metal: Volume 3: The Nineties, Ye Olde Metal: 1968 to 1972*

2006: *Run for Cover: The Art of Derek Riggs, Black Sabbath: Doom Let Loose, Dio: Light Beyond the Black*

2005: *The Collector's Guide to Heavy Metal: Volume 2: The Eighties, Rainbow: English Castle Magic, UFO: Shoot Out the Lights, The New Wave of British Heavy Metal Singles*

2004: *Blue Öyster Cult: Secrets Revealed!* (updated and reissued in 2009 with the same title; updated and reissued as *Agents of Fortune: The Blue Öyster Cult Story* in 2016), *Contents Under Pressure: 30 Years of Rush at Home & Away, The Top 500 Heavy Metal Albums of All Time*

2003: *The Collector's Guide to Heavy Metal: Volume 1: The Seventies, The Top 500 Heavy Metal Songs of All Time*

2001: *Southern Rock Review*

2000: *Heavy Metal: 20th Century Rock and Roll, The Goldmine Price Guide to Heavy Metal Records*

1997: *The Collector's Guide to Heavy Metal*

1993: *Riff Kills Man! 25 Years of Recorded Hard Rock & Heavy Metal*

See martinpopoff.com for complete details and ordering information.

IMAGE CREDITS

INDEX

Quarto.com

© 2025 Quarto Publishing Group USA Inc.
Text © 2025 Martin Popoff

First Published in 2025 by Motorbooks, an imprint
of The Quarto Group,
100 Cummings Center, Suite 265-D, Beverly, MA
01915, USA.
T (978) 282-9590 F (978) 283-2742

Motorbooks titles are also available at discount for
retail, wholesale, promotional, and bulk purchase.
For details, contact the Special Sales Manager by
email at specialsales@quarto.com or by mail at The
Quarto Group, Attn: Special Sales Manager, 100
Cummings Center, Suite 265-D, Beverly, MA 01915,
USA.

29 28 27 26 25   1 2 3 4 5

ISBN: 978-0-7603-9399-4

Digital edition published in 2025
eISBN: 978-0-7603-9400-7

Library of Congress Cataloging-in-Publication Data

Names: Popoff, Martin, 1963- author.
Title: Guns n' Roses at 40 / Martin Popoff.
Description: Beverly, MA : Motorbooks, 2025. |
Includes index. | Summary:
  "Guns N' Roses at 40 is an engaging look back at
the career of the
  sometimes controversial, always entertaining rock
band"-- Provided by
  publisher.
Identifiers: LCCN 2024046244 | ISBN
9780760393994 | ISBN 9780760394007
  (ebook)
Subjects: LCSH: Rock musicians--United States--
Biography. | Guns n' Roses
  (Musical group) | Rock musicians--United States-
-Biography.
Classification: LCC ML421.G86 P66 2025 | DDC
782.42166092/2
  [B]--dc23/eng/20241001
LC record available at https://lccn.loc.
gov/2024046244

Design and layout: Burge Agency

Printed in Malaysia